"The repackaging of classics is a tried and trusted winner, but Tim Coates has come up with something entirely original: the repackaging of history. His **uncovered editions** collect papers from the archive of The Stationery Office into verbatim narratives, so, for instance, in UFOs in the House of Lords we get a hilarious recreation, directly from Hansard, of a nutty debate that took place in 1979 . . . This is inspired publishing, not only archivally valuable but capable of bringing the past back to life without the usual filter of academic or biographer." **Guardian**

"The Irish Uprising is a little treasure of a book and anyone with an interest in Irish history will really enjoy it. Its structure is extremely unusual as it is compiled from historic official reports published by the British government from 1914 to 1920 . . . For anyone studying this period of history The Irish Uprising is a must as the correspondence and accounts within it are extremely illuminating and the subtle nuances of meaning can be teased out of the terms and phrasing to be more revelatory than the actual words themselves." **Irish Press, Belfast**

"Voyeurs of all ages will enjoy the original text of the Denning report on Profumo. It is infinitely superior to the film version of the scandal, containing such gems as: 'One night I was invited to a dinner party at the home of a very, very rich man. After I arrived, I discovered it was rather an unusual dinner party. All the guests had taken off their clothes . . . The most intriguing person was a man with a black mask over his face. At first I thought this was a party gimmick. But the truth was that this man is so well known and holds such a responsible position that he did not want to be associated with anything improper.'" **Times Higher Education Supplement**

"Very good to read . . . insight into important things . . . inexorably moving . . . If you want to read about the Titanic, you won't read a better thing . . . a revelation." **Open Book, BBC Radio 4**

"Congratulations to The Stationery Office for unearthing and reissuing such an enjoyable vignette" [on Wilfrid Blunt's Egyptian Garden] **The Spectator**

uncovered editions
www.uncovered-editions.co.uk

Series editor: Tim Coates
Managing editor: Michele Staple

New titles in the series

Already published

uncovered editions

UFOs IN AMERICA, 1947

FBI FILES RELATED TO THE SIGHTING OF UNIDENTIFIED FLYING OBJECTS DURING 1947

∘⋘⋙∘

London: The Stationery Office

Applications for reproduction should be made in writing to The Stationery Office Limited, St Crispins, Duke Street, Norwich NR3 1PD.

ISBN 0 11 702746 4
Extracts taken from the files of the Federal Bureau of Investigation, available under the Freedom of Information Act.

A CIP catalogue record for this book is available from the British Library.

Cover photograph of a group of curious US citizens scanning the night sky for UFOs.
© Bettmann/CORBIS.

Typeset by J&L Composition Ltd, Filey, North Yorkshire.

Printed in the United Kingdom by The Stationery Office, London.
TJ5455 C20 10/01

CONTENTS

The modern UFO era started in 1947, when nine "flying saucers" were reported having been seen in the sky near Mount Rainier in the USA. Although it is estimated that up to 98 per cent of UFOs have straightforward explanations, including meteors, lightning effects or weather kites and balloons (hoaxes constitute only a small fraction of reports), it is the remaining unexplained phenomena which have gripped the public imagination. Sightings have been recorded since ancient times.

This selection of documents, from the FBI's vast files on the subject, offer an insight into the prevailing mood during the Cold War. The reader may also find interest in UFOs in the House of Lords, 1979 *in this series.*

Due to the fragile condition of the original material, some of the documents may contain discrepancies or omissions, although every effort has been made to rectify these.
Note that the symbol (X) indicates a word or passage that has not been released under the Freedom of Information Act.

From the Irish Annals, reported in the Census of 1851

AD 745 "In the night a terrible and wonderful sign appeared amongst the stars."

AD 745 "Dragons were seen in the sky."

AD 745 Eclipses of the moon in June and December.

AD 746 "Serpents were seen in the sky."

AD 747 "Snow of unusual depth, so that almost all the cattle of Ireland were destroyed."

AD 748 "Ships, with their sailors, were seen in the air over Cluainmicnose."

AD 748 "Ships were seen in the air in Donnell MacMurrough's reign."

AD 748 "Snow of unusual depth, so that almost all the cattle of the whole of Ireland were destroyed; and afterwards the world was parched with unusual dryness. Ships with their crews were seen in the air."

AD 749 "The moon was of a sanguine colour."

AD 752 "An eclipse of the sun."

AD 753 "The sun was darkened. The moon was suffused with bloody red this year."

JUNE, 1947

Note that the following documents, although written in July, refer to a UFO sighting on June 24, 1947, and therefore have been grouped under this month.

Office memorandum of the US Government to Director FBI. Attention: D. M. Ladd

From: SAC [Special Agent in Charge], San Francisco
Subject: Flying discs   July 28, 1947
There is transmitted herewith for the information of the Bureau a report received from Lieutenant

(X), A-2, Hamilton Field, California, containing the results of an investigation by his office concerning the reported sighting of flying discs.

In addition to containing the detailed descriptions of what was allegedly seen by several persons, the Bureau's attention is particularly called to the first memorandum setting forth the notes of Agent (X), CIC, Fourth Air Force, concerning an interview he had with Mr (X), Box 387, Boise, Idaho, on July 12, 1947, who reported that he had seen nine strange objects flying over the Cascade Mountain Range of Washington State. It will be noted that the CIC Agent reports that "Mr (X) is very outspoken and somewhat bitter in his opinions of the leaders of the United States Army Air Forces and the FBI for not having made an investigation of this matter sooner."

The thought has occurred to me that the Bureau might desire to have an agent of the Butte Office contact Mr (X) and explain to him our lack of jurisdiction in such matters.

Investigation made at Palm Springs, California, Boise, Idaho and Hamilton Field, California

Title: Flying discs   July 18, 1947
Controlling Office: Air Defense Command; period covered: 10 July 47 to 18 July 47; reason for investigation initiated at the request of Head-

quarters Air Defense Command, reference letter Headquarters Air Defense Command, dated July 7, 47, subject: investigation of flying discs.

Synopsis:
Flying discs first reported in this area June 24, 1947 near Mount Rainier, Washington, by (X); unidentified object reported July 9, 1947 at approximately 1277 near Boise, Idaho by (X), *Idaho Daily Statesman*; unidentified objects reported by (X), United Air Lines Pilot, July 4, 1947, 8 minutes out of Boise, Idaho; record check of law enforcement agencies, public utilities and local residences revealed no record of (X) in Palm Springs; unidentified objects reported July 8, 1947 at 1245, travelling northeast over Hamilton Field by (X); unidentified objects reported over Grand Canyon, Arizona, 0910 MST by (X), USM and in vicinity of Lake Meade by (X), HQ, Tenth Air Force, Brooks Field, Texas; extent of publicity in local area indicated by press clippings.

LIEUTENANT (X)
Headquarters Fourth Air Force
Office of the Assistant Chief of Staff A-2
Hamilton Field, California

Memorandum for the officer in charge

On July 12, 1947, (X) of Boise, Idaho was interviewed in regard to the report that he saw nine
strange objects flying over the Cascade Mountain
Range of Washington State on June 24. (X) volun-
tarily agreed to give the interviewer a written
report of exactly what he had seen on the above-
mentioned date [see p. 6].

Agent's notes:
(X) is a man of 32 years of age, being married and
the father of two children. He is well thought of in
the community in which he lives, being very much
the family man and from all appearances a very
good provider for his family. (X) has recently purchased an airplane in which to conduct his business. It is the personal opinion of the interviewer
that (X) actually saw what he stated he saw. It is difficult to believe that a man of his character and
apparent integrity would state that he saw objects
and write up a report to the extent that he did if
he did not see them. To go further, if he can write
a report of the character that he did while not having seen the objects that he claimed he saw, it is the
opinion of the interviewer that (X) is in the wrong
business, that he should be writing Buck Rogers
fiction. (X) is very outspoken and somewhat bitter
in his opinions of the leaders of the US Army Air
Forces and the FBI for not having made an

investigation of this matter sooner. To put all of the statements made by him in this report would make it a voluminous volume. However, after having checked an aeronautical map of the area over which he claims that he saw the objects, it was determined that all statements made by him in regard to the distances involved, speed of the objects, course of the objects and size of the objects, could very possibly be facts. The distances mentioned by (X) in his report are within a short distance of the actual distances on aeronautical charts of this area, although he has never consulted aeronautical charts of the type the Army uses. He stated that his business had suffered greatly since his report on June 25 due to the fact that at every stop on his business routes, large crowds of people were waiting to question him as to just what he had seen. (X) stated further that if he, at any time in the future, saw anything in the sky, to quote him directly, "If I saw a ten-story building flying through the air I would never say a word about it," due to the fact that he has been ridiculed by the press to such an extent that he is practically a moron in the eyes of the majority of the population of the United States.

Some life data on (X):
My flying experiences started as a boy in Minot, North Dakota, where I took my first flying lesson. Due to the high cost at that time, I was unable to continue my flying and did not fly of any great

consequence until 1943. I was given my pilot certificate by the senior CAA inspector of Portland, Oregon, and for the last (X), covering my entire territory with same and flying from 40 to 100 hours per month since. Due to the fact that I use an airplane entirely in my work, in January of this year I purchased an airplane designed for high-altitude take-offs and short rough field usage.

In the type of flying I do, it takes a great deal of practice and judgment to be able to land in most any cow pasture and get out without injuring your airplane; the runways are very limited and the altitude is very high in some of the fields and places I have to go in my work. To date, I have landed in 832 cow pastures in mountain meadows, and in over 1,000 hours a flat tire has been my greatest mishap.

Report of incident:
The following story of what I observed over the Cascade Mountains, as impossible as it may seem, is positively true. I never asked nor wanted any notoriety for just accidentally being in the right spot at the right time to observe what I did. I reported something that I know any pilot would have reported. I don't think that in any way my observation was due to any sensitivity of eyesight or judgement than what is considered normal for any pilot.

On June 24, Tuesday, 1947, I had finished my work at Ghehalis, Washington, and at about 2 o'clock I took off from Ghehalis, Washington, airport with the intention of going to Yakima, Washington. My trip was delayed for an hour to search for a larger transport that supposedly went down near or around the southwest side of Mount Rainier in the state of Washington and to date has never been found.

I flew directly toward Mount Rainier after reaching an altitude of about 9,500 feet, which is the approximate elevation of the high plateau from which Mount Rainier rises. I had made one sweep of this high plateau to the westward, searching all of the various ridges for this marine ship and flew to the west down and near the ridge side of the canyon where Ashford, Washington, is located.

Unable to see anything that looked like the lost ship, I made a 300-degree turn to the right and above the little city of Mineral, starting again toward Mount Rainier. I climbed back up to an altitude of approximately 9,200 feet.

The air was so smooth that day that it was a real pleasure flying and, as most pilots do when the air is smooth and they are flying at a higher altitude, I trimmed out [balanced] my airplane in the direction of Yakima, Washington, which was almost directly east of my position and simply sat in my plane observing the sky and the terrain. There was a DC-4 to the left and to the rear of me approximately 15 miles distant, and I should judge, at 14,000 feet elevation. The sky and air were as clear

as crystal. I had not flown more than 2 or 3 minutes on my course when a bright flash reflected on
my airplane. It startled me as I thought I was too
close to some other aircraft. I looked every place in
the sky and couldn't find where the reflection had
come from until I looked to the left end of Mount
Rainier where I observed a chain of nine peculiar-
looking aircraft flying from north to south at
approximately 9,500 feet elevation and going,
seemingly, in a definite direction of about 170
degrees north to south.

They were approaching Mount Rainier very
rapidly, and I merely assumed they were jet planes.
Anyhow, I discovered that this was where the
reflection had come from, as two or three of them
every few seconds would dip or change their course
slightly, just enough for the sun to strike them at
an angle that reflected brightly on my plane.

These objects being quite far away, I was unable
for a few seconds to make out their shape or their
formation. Very shortly they approached Mount
Rainier, and I observed their outline against the
snow quite plainly.

I thought it was very peculiar that I couldn't
find their tails but assumed they were some type of
jet plane. I was determined to clock their speed, as
I had two definite points I could clock them by;
the air was so clear that it was very easy to see
objects and determine their approximate shape and
size at almost 50 miles that day.

I remember distinctly that my sweep-second hand on my eight-day clock, which is located on my instrument panel, read one minute to 3 pm as the first object of this formation passed the southern edge of Mount Rainier. I watched these objects with great interest as I had never before observed airplanes flying so close to the mountaintops, flying directly south to southeast down the hog's back of a mountain range. I would estimate their elevation could have varied 1,000 feet one way or another up or down, but they were pretty much on the horizon to me which would indicate they were near the same elevation as I was.

They flew like many times I have observed geese to fly in a diagonal-like line as if they were linked together. They seemed to hold a definite direction but rather swerved in and out of the high mountain peaks. Their speed at the time did not impress me particularly, because I knew that our army and air forces had planes that went very fast.

What kept bothering me as I watched them flip and flash in the sun right along their path was the fact that I couldn't make out any tail in them, and I am sure that any pilot would justify more than a second look at such a plane.

I observed them quite plainly, and I estimate my distance from them, which was almost at right angles, to be between 20 to 25 miles. I knew they must be very large to observe their shape at that distance, even on as clear a day as it was that Tuesday. In fact, I compared a zeus fastener or cowling tool [used for adjusting hood of airplane] I had in my pocket — holding it up on them and holding it up on the DC-4 — that I could observe at quite a distance to my left — and they seemed to be smaller than the DC-4 but I should judge their span would have been as wide as the furtherest engines on each side of the fuselage of the DC-4.

The more I observed these objects, the more upset I became, as I am accustomed and familiar with most all objects flying whether I am close to the ground or at higher altitude. I observed the chain of these objects passing another high snow-covered ridge in between Mount Rainier and Mount Adams, and as the first one was passing the south crest of this ridge, the last object was entering the northern crest of the ridge.

As I was flying in the direction of this particular ridge, I measured it and found it to be approximately 5 miles, so I could safely assume that the chain of these saucer-like objects was about 5 miles long. I could quite accurately determine their pathway due to the fact that there were several high peaks that were a little this side of them as well as higher peaks on the other side of their pathway.

As the last unit of this formation passed the southernmost high snow-covered crest of Mount Adams, I looked at my sweep-second hand and it showed that they had traveled the distance in 1

minute and 42 seconds. Even at the time this tim-
ing did not upset me, as I felt confident after I
landed there would be some explanation of what I
saw.

A number of newsmen and experts suggested
that I might have been seeing reflections or even a
mirage. This I know to be absolutely false, as I
observed these objects not only through the glass
of my airplane but turned my airplane sideways
where I could open my window to observe them
with a completely unobstructed view (without
sunglasses).

Even though 2 minutes seems like a very short
time to one on the ground, in the air in 2 minutes
a pilot can observe a great many things and anything within his sight of vision probably as many as
50 or 60 times.

I continued my search for the marine plane for
another 15 or 20 minutes and while searching for
this marine plane, what I had just observed kept
going through my mind. I became more disturbed,
so after taking a last look at Tieton Reservoir I
headed for Yakima.

I might add that my complete observation of
these objects, which I could even follow by their
flashes as they passed Mount Adams, was around 2½
or 3 minutes — although by the time they reached
Mount Adams they were out of my range of vision
as far as determining shape or form. Of course,
when the sun reflected from one or two or three of

these units, they appeared to be completely round; but I am making a drawing to the best of my ability as to the shape I observed these objects to be as they passed the snow-covered ridges as well as Mount Rainier.

When these objects were flying approximately straight and level, they were just a black thin line and when they flipped was the only time I could get a judgement as to their size. These objects were holding an almost constant elevation; they did not seem to be going up or to be going down, such as would be the case of rockets or artillery shells. I am convinced in my own mind that they were some type of airplane, even though they didn't conform with the many aspects of the conventional type of planes that I know.

Although these objects have been reported by many other observers throughout the United States, there have been six or seven other accounts written by some of these observers that I can truthfully say must have observed the same thing that I did; particularly, the description of the three Western Air Lines employees of Cedar City, Utah; the pilot from Oklahoma City and the locomotive engineer in Illinois, plus (X) and co-pilot (X) of United Air Lines.

Some descriptions could not be very accurate taken from the ground unless these saucer-like disks were at quite a great height and there is a possibility that all of the people who observed peculiar objects could have seen the same thing that I did; but it would have been very difficult from the ground to observe these for more than 4 or 5 seconds, and there is always the possibility of atmospheric moisture and dust near the ground which could distort one's vision.

I have in my possession letters from all over the United States and people who profess that these objects have been observed over other portions of the world, principally Sweden, Bermuda and California.

I would have given almost anything that day to have had a movie camera with telephoto lens and from now on I will never be without one — but, to continue further with my story. When I landed at the Yakima, Washington, airport I described what I had seen to my very good friend, Al Baxter, who listened patiently and was very courteous but in a joking way didn't believe me.

I did not accurately measure the distance between these two mountains until I landed at Pendleton, Oregon, that same day where I told a number of pilot friends of mine what I observed and they did not scoff or laugh but suggested they might be guided missiles or something new. In fact, several former Army pilots informed me that they had been briefed before going into combat overseas that they might see objects of similar shape and design as I described and assured me that I wasn't dreaming or going crazy.

I quote (X), a former Army Air Forces pilot: "What you observed, I am convinced, is some type of jet- or rocket-propelled ship that is in the process of being tested by our government or even it could possibly be by some foreign government".

Anyhow, the news that I had observed these spread very rapidly and before night was over I was receiving telephone calls from all parts of the world; and, to date I have not received one telephone call or one letter that was scoffing or disbelief. The only disbelief that I know of was what was printed in the papers.

I look at this whole ordeal as not something funny as some people have made it out to be. To me it is mighty serious and since I evidently did observe something that at least Mr John Doe on the street corner or Pete Andrews on the ranch has never heard about, is no reason that it does not exist.

Even though I openly invited an investigation by the Army and the FBI as to the authenticity of my story or a physical examination as to my capabilities, I received no interest from those two important protective forces of our country. I will go so far as to assume that any report I gave to the United and Associated Press and over the radio on two different occasions which apparently set the nation buzzing, if our Military Intelligence was not aware of what I observed, they would be the very first people I could expect as visitors.

I have received lots of requests from people who told me to make a lot of wild guesses. I have based what I have written here in this article on positive facts and as far as guessing what it was I observed, it is just as much a mystery to me as it is to the rest of the world.

JULY, 1947: NEWSPAPER EXTRACTS

[*Washington Post*, July 7, 1947]

PRIEST FINDS "WHIRRING" DISC IN YARD AND HOLDS IT FOR FBI

Chicago, July 6. A Catholic priest at Grafton, Wisconsin, said tonight that a round metal disc which might be one of the mysterious flying saucers had crashed into his parish yard and that he is holding it for the Federal Bureau of Investigation.

The Rev. Joseph Brasky of St Joseph's Church at Grafton, 45 miles north of Milwaukee, said he heard a swishing and whirring noise this morning. A second later he said he heard a thud and a mild explosion.

He investigated and found a sheet metal disc about 18″ in diameter in the middle of the disc, he said, and in the opening were "gadgets and some wires". The priest said he did not know if his discovery were important or whether it might be an elaborate practical joke. He said he had notified the FBI of his find. H. K. Johnson of the Milwaukee FBI office said he hadn't heard yet about the disc but that an official report might be at his office.

The flying discs have been reported "seen" by persons in 30 states, but Brasky's disc was the first one that actually had been found — if that is what was found. His report came a few hours after a military plane made an unsuccessful speed dash in an attempt to track down one of the discs and the Army and scientists sought to ascertain whether coast-to-coast reports about the discs zooming through the sky were fact or fancy. Army planes scoured the northwest Pacific skies for them without success today and one "eyewitness" even reported having seen one of the discs take off in Arizona. A St Louis railroad man exhibited some paper "discs" he said he had seen floating over St Louis.

The flying saucers which have been reported skimming through America's skies at speeds up to

1,200 miles have eluded the usually keen eye of radar.
Capt. Tom Brown of the Army Air Forces public relations staff said the Army Airways Communications
Service had reported late yesterday that so far its radar
scopes throughout the country have been unable to
pick up any strange objects in flight. And in the Pacific
Northwest — where most of the fly-happy platters
have been reported — the Army has radar equipment
which can pierce fog and darkness and pick up objects
in the sky 200 miles away. Even so, Brown acknowledged that the Air Forces had decided "there's
something to this" and had been checking it for 10
days. "And we still haven't the slightest idea what they
could be," he added.

And a new wrinkle — the reported landing of
a fleet of eight skimming platters — was reported
from Idaho in full view of 10 persons. A. Dishman,
Idaho housewife, said she and others in her party
had seen the saucers land on a mountainside near
St Maries, Idaho. She said they came into view at
an extreme speed, suddenly slowed, and then "fluttered like leaves to the ground. The mysterious part
was that we couldn't see them after they landed,"
she said. "We could see them flutter down into the
timber yet we couldn't see that they did anything
to the trees." She said she hoped to hike into the
timber tomorrow and search for the objects which
she said were saucer-shaped but resembled wash-
tubs more than disks and were "about the size of a
five-room house".

Locally, Hazen Kennedy of 2615 4th Street reported he had seen one passing over the northeast section of the city at about 8.40 pm. This would be the first one reported over the district, although others have been reported over nearby Maryland. Kennedy, who has 125 hours flying time as a student pilot in the Army Air Forces to his credit, said he believed the saucer he had seen was traveling at "well over" 1,000 mph at an altitude of between 1,200 and 1,500 feet. "The best way I can describe it," said Kennedy, "was that it looked like an orange lamp bulb without the socket. It was goin' faster than any jet plane I've ever seen."

In Hagerstown, Mrs Madelyn Ganoe, 30, said she had seen five of the discs, racing in 2–1–2 formation at "terrific speed" from her back porch. "They sounded like a faraway train," she said.

In the wake of these new eyewitness accounts came a new series of comments and explanations, but most of them were tinged with a slight tendency to laugh off the whole thing. Dr Winfred Overholser, nationally known psychiatrist and superintendent of St Elizabeth's Hospital here, said it "has some of the earmarks of being national hysteria. Every time someone comes up with a sea-serpent story," said Dr Overholser, "others with vivid imaginations are sure they have seen the same thing. The critical faculty in man, the last one he received, is still not very well developed. Scratch the surface and you will find the same mass hysteria which predominated during the witchcraft scare. Some persons are quite ready to see things and follow beliefs." Dr Overholser said that when he made his rounds of the mental patients yesterday at St Elizabeth's, not one commented on the flying saucers story. "I think they may be a little sceptical," he added.

However, Dr Overholser said he wasn't trying to dismiss the matter as a joke "because there are so many strange things going on today that one can't be sure."

Major Alexander P. de Seversky, noted aircraft designer, told the *Post* by telephone from New York that until he sees a flying saucer he "wouldn't like to pass judgement." He agreed with Dr Overholser that much if not all of the story may be because of hysteria. "After all," he said, "we are more or less an hysterical nation." Major de Seversky said it was possible that the persons who claim to have seen the aerial discs have instead glimpsed the exhaust of jet-propelled planes. He conceded, too, that they might be guided missiles let loose as part of an experiment, but added: "I don't think the Government would fire them so promiscuously. They would test them in one spot, in an isolated area, like they did the atomic bomb."

Major General Curtis E. LeMay, who, as Deputy Chief of Air Staff for Research and Development would know if the saucers involved experiments with guided missiles, commented: "Whatever these people have seen it hasn't been anything resulting from experiments by the Army Air Forces. As far as I'm concerned there's nothing to it at all. The whole thing is unfortunate."

However, Nova Hart, St Louis mechanic who was trained during service in the war to spot all types of aircraft, yesterday offered a minute description of one of the flying patterns which he claimed he saw flying at an altitude of about 300 feet. He described it as circular with a ribbed framework and silver-gray in color. He said it appeared to have a motor with a propeller attached in the center and that it kept turning like an airplane doing a slow roll.

Although many explanations have been offered, none has been convincing. A Los Angeles newspaper quoted an unnamed nuclear physicist as saying the silvery discs resulted from experiments in the "transmutation of atomic energy". This report was rapidly herded into the hoax column by David Lilienthal, chairman of the Atomic Energy Commission, and several prominent atomic scientists.

Louis E. Starr, national commander of the Veterans of Foreign Wars, announced Saturday at Columbus, Ohio, that he was expecting "momentarily" information from Washington which would explain the dashing discs. But the message never arrived.

The Air Forces said that General Carl Spaatz, Air Forces chief, was in the Pacific Northwest where most of the saucers have been reported, but added that his trip there was planned two months ago, long before the saucers scare. General Spaatz is expected back in Washington late tomorrow.

Muroc Army Air Field in California had a P-80 jet fighter standing by, and the National Guard in Oregon had prepared six regular fighters to give chase should saucers be reported nearby.

[*Birmingham News*, July 7, 1947]

FLYING SAUCERS REPORTED FROM 39 STATES BUT SEEM TO BE CONCENTRATED HERE

City is baffled by dazzling display of spooky discs

The strange things that have been in night skies since June 25 were over Birmingham last night.

On one thing everyone who has seen the mysterious objects agree — they are round, saucer-like. After that, every story differs. Each of the hundreds of callers who reported witnessing the baffling sky demonstrations had a different version of what they saw.

Some said the objects were large, some small. They were moving at great speed. They were suspended in the air. There was sound along with their movements. They moved noiselessly through the black sky. They were at great distance from the earth.

They had fallen to the ground. They were in perfect formation. They were colliding with each other.

But whatever the things are that have set the nation agog since first reported 12 days ago by a man in Washington state, they definitely went over the Magic City last night. It seems, in fact, that more Birmingham residents saw the objects than in any other place.

Reports began coming into the *Age-Herald* city room around 8 o'clock last night. For more than an hour thereafter the place was bedlam. The switchboard operators were swamped with calls.

[*Milwaukee Journal*, July 7, 1947]

PRIEST HEARS A "BANG", DISCOVERS A CIRCULAR BLADE WITH TEETH; OTHER DISKS "SEEN" BY MILWAUKEEANS

The "what is it?" which Father Joseph Brasky said he found early Sunday on the lawn of St Joseph's Catholic church in Grafton may be just another gadget to add to Father Brasky's already sizeable collection.

Those who saw it Sunday said "what is it?" was a circular saw blade with a few wires attached. Father Brasky, who said he knew of no sawmills in the area, would not claim it was a "flying saucer" when he called newspapermen to his home. "It may or may not be one of those flying disks that have been reported all over the country," he said. "Let's just call it a 'what is it?'"

Meanwhile, in Milwaukee and other points in Wisconsin, several persons reported seeing the "flying saucers". Father Brasky's disk, however, was the only case here in which the "landing" of a "saucer" was reported. Father Brasky gave the following account of how he found the object, a steel plate 19″ in diameter, about ⅛″ thick and with saw teeth.

> I usually get up about 5 am on Sundays. I was at the front door of my house, about to take my dog out for a walk, when I heard a "bang!" like a big firecracker. I stepped outside and found this disk on the church lawn. Although the grass was still wet from the night rain, the disk was too hot to pick up. I noticed the glass ball had been knocked off one of the lightning rods on the church, so I suppose it struck that in landing.

Father Brasky said he did not bother to show the disk to any of his parishioners on Sunday. He tried to telephone an FBI agent whom he knows, but was unable to reach him Sunday, he added. Asked whether it could have been the work of a practical joker, Father Brasky replied: "Could be. I don't know . . ."

The disk, apparently of steel, had a 1⅜″ hole in the center. Through it ran a few wires. To each end of the cluster of wires was attached what looked like small condenser about 3″ long. The condenser-like objects were wrapped in black tape which still was sticky. The disk was greasy and somewhat dirty. Stamped on it was "Approved, Dunlap".

Father Brasky declined to part with the disk. He showed a number of items in his trinket collection. All of them had something to do with fishing, Father Brasky's favorite sport. They included his "bass bottles"— beer bottles with the head of a fish — and a fish pole from Manila which folds up into a cane. When opened, it extends to 12 feet. "I use it in reaching folks who can't be touched with a 10 foot pole," Father Brasky quipped.

Father Brasky also passed out copies of his recent publication, *Fish Tales*. "I'm going to revise this thing," he explained. "I've got some new and better tales to put in it."

There were other reports around Milwaukee and Wisconsin of "flying saucers". Mrs Anthony Hoffman, 3410 W. Layton Avenue, said she and her husband saw one at 8.25 pm Sunday flying toward Billy Mitchell Field from the northwest. When it neared the field, it veered towards the south and disappeared, she said. It was flying high and appeared illuminated, according to Mrs Hoffman. "It looked like a small meat platter," Mrs Hoffman asserted.

Glenn Rowden of Detroit claimed he saw a "saucer", about 50″ in diameter, over Billy Mitchell

Field at 10.05 pm when he alighted from an airplane. He said it was in sight for 90 seconds.

William Humphrey, who lives with his wife in
a quonset [prefab] hut at 3148 S. 20th Street, telephoned police at 9 pm Sunday that he and Mrs
Humphrey had seen a slightly illuminated disk
which appeared to fall to earth near Pulaski high
school. Mrs Humphrey said Monday that her husband tried unsuccessfully to photograph the disk.

Erwin Rottman, 1328 N. 19th Street, claimed
he saw three of them flying through the air in a
northwesterly direction at 6 pm on Sunday. They
turned from orange to gold to silver before disappearing, he said.

Reports came also from Janesville, where Mr
and Mrs Alva Sievert and Mr and Mrs Howard Roth
reported seeing a flying disk at about 11.35 pm
Saturday. The Roths were leaving the Sievert home
when Sievert saw it, according to Roth. It appeared
to be several thousand feet up and about 10 miles
away, Roth said. He described it as vaguely resembling the moon and as having a regular motion in a
counter-clockwise, elongated orbit. It appeared to
Roth to be moving faster than an airplane. He said
it was yellow on its face, but when it turned it
looked silver. Roth said that the four of them
viewed the disk for 10 minutes. "It fluttered around,
faded out and came back again. And once it just
stopped and hung there for about two minutes,"
Roth said. "The last time we saw it, it had a very

noticeable tail. When it disappeared entirely, it just popped out."

Janesville police reported a telephone call from a Dick Thompson, who said he saw flying disks about 12.15 am Sunday.

At Oshkosh, Mrs L. A. Davis reported that she and her husband had sighted one of the mysterious disks whizzing over the city at 6.45 pm Sunday. She said they were driving on a town road 6 miles west of Oshkosh, headed east toward the city, when they first sighted the object "flying very fast and very high". At first, she said, it looked like an airplane and then loomed larger and larger until it "appeared as big as the sun." Her husband stopped the car so that they could get a better look at the disk, which appeared round and silvery, but by the time they got out of the car the object had disappeared, she said.

At Green Bay, Eugene Le Plant reported that he and his 12-year-old son, Duane, had seen a rapidly moving silver ball or disk about 6.30 pm Wednesday while working in his garden on the western edge of the city. Le Plant said he saw the object silhouetted against a dark cloud to the north and that he and his son watched it for three or four minutes while it moved away to the northwest. Le Plant said he could not estimate the altitude or distance, but that it "definitely was not an airplane."

[*Milwaukee Sentinel*, July 7, 1947]

"FLYING SAUCERS" SEEN IN 36 STATES; JET FIGHTERS ALERTED

San Francisco, July 6. Military aircraft hunted the skies over Pacific Coast states today for sight of the mysterious "flying saucers" that for 12 days have puzzled the entire country. Early reports of results were negative.

Five P-51s of the Oregon National Guard cruised over the Cascade Mountains of Washington — the area where the strange objects first were reported sighted. A sixth circled over Portland, in constant radio contact with the other five. All carried photographic equipment. Col. G. R. Dodson, commanding, described their flight as a "routine patrol", but said they had been instructed to watch for the flying discs.

At Manhattan Beach, California, A. W. McKelvey took a Mustang fighter plane up above Van Nuys. For two hours he cruised at 35,000 feet, but "didn't see a thing". Gen. Carl Spaatz, commandant of the Army Air Forces, was on a Pacific Northwest fishing trip. He denied knowing anything about the flying discs — or of plans to use AAF planes to look for them. "I've been out of touch with things for four or five days," he said. Louis E. Starr, national commander-in-chief of the Veterans of Foreign Wars, yesterday in Columbus, Oregon, said he understood Spaatz had a "group out right now" looking for discs. At Muroc Army Air Field in California a P-80 jet fighter stood ready to take off the moment any flying saucers are sighted in that area.

A cautious attitude marked both official and scientific comments, but Capt. Tom Brown of the Air Forces Public Relations staff in Washington acknowledged the Air Forces had decided "there's something to this" and had been checking up on it for 10 days.

First sighted June 25 and greeted generally with scornful laughs, the objects have been reported every day since by observers in 36 states. Most of the objects were reported seen on July 4. A few were reported yesterday. Such competent observers as airline pilots said they had seen the totally unexplained discs or saucers, larger than aircraft and flying in "loose formation" at high speed.

David Lillienthal, chairman of the Atomic Energy Commission, said they had nothing to do with atomic experiments, and Army and Navy offi-cials also entered positive disclaimers. Newspaper stories quoting an unidentified California Institute of Technology scientist as saying the phenomena might have something to do with experiments in "transmutation of atomic energy" caused a brief sensation late yesterday. The institute quickly denied the report.

Reports generally agreed that the flying objects were round or oval. Estimates of their speed ranged from about 300 to 1,200 miles an hour. They were described as flying with an undulating motion at heights of 10,000 feet and less. Some described them as glowing, or luminous.

Nova Hart, St Louis mechanic who was trained during service in the war to spot all types of aircraft, said he saw one of the strange objects near Pattonville yesterday. It was flying at 300 feet, he said. He described it as circular, with a ribbed framework and silver-gray in color. Hart said it appeared to have a motor with a propeller attached in the center and it kept turning like an airplane doing a slow roll.

First published reports of the phenomena occurred June 25. Kenneth Arnold, Boise, Idaho, businessman pilot, told of seeing nine of the discs flying in formation at 1,200 miles an hour over the Cascade Mountains in Washington. Arnold's account was taken lightly. Various explanations were offered — "reflections", "persistent vision", "snow blindness". Soon afterward other individuals — in New Mexico, Missouri, California and other states — reported they also had seen the flying objects.

Then on Independence Day 200 persons in one group and 60 in another saw them in Idaho. Hundreds of others in Oregon, Washington and other western states reported seeing them. July 4 also brought first reports of the flying discs from east of the Mississippi. Since then they have been reported seen in widely separated sections of the country — in 33 states in all.

London, July 6 (Associated Press). Don't mention those flying saucers on this side of the Atlantic unless you're prepared for an argument about your sanity.

Maybe they have been seen by sober citizens over a vast area of the United States, but Europe won't believe in them until somebody lassoes one and has it photographed by Frank Sinatra, the British ambassador and five Supreme Court justices. "America's reply to the Loch Ness monster," chortled today's Sunday dispatch, referring to Britain's hoariest tall story — the serpent that is "seen" romping in Scotland's Loch Ness every time the tourist trade needs a shot in the arm.

[*Milwaukee Journal*, July 7, 1947]

PLANES CHASING DISKS FIND ONLY EMPTY SKY

Jokesters add some comedy to air mystery

Army pilots were ready Monday for another air search for the mysterious "flying saucers" now reported seen in 39 states and parts of Canada, as practical jokesters added to the confusion.

Equipped with telescopic cameras, 11 army planes searched the Pacific Northwest Sunday without finding any trace of the flying disks which had been reported over scores of communities the preceding two days. At Sioux Falls, South Dakota, a national guard plane already in the air was ordered to investigate a silvery disk with a short tail which Gregory Zimmer said he saw shoot across the heavens. The pilot found nothing but empty sky. The army "camera patrol" over the Cascade Mountains Sunday included eight P-51 Pursuit ships and three A-26 bombers.

There was growing belief that the concentrated aerial search would show the saucers to be optical illusions or the work of practical jokesters magnified by aroused imaginations. A number of "disks" whirled over rooftops in East St Louis, Illinois, Sunday. J. T. Hartley, a locomotive engineer, gathered some of them up and found they were made of pressed white paper, 11″ in diameter and with a 2″ hole in the center. Railroad workers said they looked like locomotive packing washers.

A radio announcement that disks were flying over Lewiston, Idaho, Sunday sent hundreds into their yards for a look. Weatherman Louis Krezak said the objects were moving eastward with the prevailing wind and probably were weed seeds. Three air transport pilots agreed.

A Birmingham radio station was deluged with more than 400 calls in one hour by persons who said they saw fluorescent balls circling over the city and clearly outlined against nearby mountains. A carnival at Alabaster, Alabama, was playing search-lights on cloud wisps.

An argument raged at Lodi, California, over the cause of a spectacular glow in the sky and a roar shortly before electrical power went off. Mrs W. C. Smith said she heard a noise "like a four-motored bomber" just before the lights went off at dawn. Erving Newcomb of the Pacific Gas & Electric Co. offered the explanation that a low-flying crop dusting plane probably had struck a power line and burned out a transformer. However, no planes were reported damaged and no one could explain what a crop dusting plane was doing in the air at dawn on Sunday. It was the first time any noise had been attributed to flying saucers.

J.U. Watts, Jr, Darlington, South Carolina attorney, said he saw an army pursuit plane chasing a V-formation of flying saucers at 250 miles an hour 3,000 feet high. However, no pilot reported such a chase.

Meantime, authorities were plagued with reports that bordered on the fantastic. An excited Chicago woman reported that she had seen a flying saucer with legs. "I was standing on my porch and I thought for sure it was coming right down and slap me in the face," she said. George Kuger of Denver said he saw a flying disk with an American flag on it. Francis Howell, Tempe, Arizona, claimed he saw a saucer 2 feet in diameter disappear behind a row of trees near his home. When he rushed to inspect it, he said, the flat, thin aluminum-like disk took off at a "high rate of speed" toward Phoenix, 9 miles away. Mrs Walter Johnson returned to Spokane, Washington, after a vacation near St Maries, Idaho, and after reading newspaper reports of the flying saucers said she and several others had seen speeding shiny objects "as big as a four- or five-room house" disappear into the forest-covered mountains.

The first of the saucers over New York State was reported by Mrs Kenneth Wohley of Rochester, New York, who said she and her husband saw an object "about the size of an ordinary saucer" flying above her back yard at 8.30 pm Sunday. New Jersey residents said they "thought" they saw flying disks over Palisades Park and nearby Bergenfield Sunday night. Sceptical scientists recalled the mysterious "rockets" seen over Sweden last year. Eighty per cent of the "ghost rockets" proved to be meteors, and Swedish officials said the others could be discounted as pure imagination.

Scientists asserted that the objects, in order to be seen clearly at 10,000 feet — the level at which most of the saucers have been reported – would have to be 20 feet in diameter, would require a large mass of metal, would be more conspicuous at night and would be seen by a far greater number of persons. Dr J. S. Nassau, director of the Warner & Swasey Observatory at the Case Institute of

Technology at Cleveland, said he was inclined to "think the reports are fancies".

Capt. Tom Brown, army air force spokesman at Washington, said the army was trying to run the reports to earth. "We're not dismissing the possibility that there's something to it," he said, "and we're not dismissing the possibility that it's all a hoax."

[*Milwaukee Sentinel*, July 7, 1947]

US PLANES HUNTING DISCS; RUSSIAN TELLS OF "ATOM SAUCERS"

FBI probes story of Soviet ship officer

Los Angeles, July 6 (Special). Federal agents today investigated a letter to the *Examiner* describing Russian supersonic atom-powered planes resembling the "flying saucers".

A top flight atomic scientist to whom the *Examiner* referred the letter said it was "not all nonsense", and suggested the matter be turned over to the FBI. The letter writer said he got the information from an officer aboard a Russian tanker recently in Los Angeles harbor. The Russian, he said, also described experiments with controlled radioactive clouds in the Arctic, where birds, animals and even worms were killed.

The planes, as described by the Russian to the writer, are only 8″ thick, with a kidney-shaped outline and no propellers. The pilot lies on his stomach and is artificially cooled against the heat developed by air friction.

"The outer surface is highly polished," the Russian said. Both upper and lower surfaces are convex, like a giant lens. The lifting force is an entirely different principle found about 10 years ago among unpublished papers of a Russian chemist. "Energy is required only for climbing, but no energy is needed for support when the airplane goes along the earth's gravitational contour lines."

The writer of the strange letter said he met the Russian officer in Wilmington and because he wanted to hear about Russia, he invited him to dinner. The Russian first asked where he could sell 18 polar bear pelts which he received "for very dangerous work". He said he had been assigned to go over the route of the radioactive cloud near Lake Baikal (or Baykal) and pick up dead animals. "They loaded a few small ships with all kinds of animals and directed the cloud over them," the writer said. "During this experiment, a violent storm blew the cloud far north into the tundra, but before it dissipated it destroyed all life on its way. The cloud may be controlled from land, from a plane or from a robot-piloted 'leader'. As I understand it, the control is based on electro-magnetic waves and the cloud has two components: the carrier and the killer."

[*Milwaukee Sentinel*, July 7, 1947]

"SAUCERS" FLY HERE

A passenger aboard a New York–Detroit–Milwaukee plane, which landed at Billy Mitchell Field at 10.05 pm, told employees in the office of Northwest Airlines, Inc., he saw a flying saucer bobbing up and down over the airfield just after he had alighted from the plane. Other passengers with him also saw it, he said. He gave the name of J.W. Rowden of Detroit. Despite its bobbing, the saucer was going at great speed, and was out of sight in a few seconds, he said. Rowden is stopping at the Plaza Hotel.

Erwin Rottman, 1328 N. 19th Street, said he saw three of them, with tails, flying northwest to southeast, as he stood at N. 18th and W. Vilet streets. They turned from gold to another color and then to silver, he said. Frank Phifer, stopping at the Maryland Hotel, said he saw three balls of fire shoot across Lake Michigan at 8.20 last night, about a mile from shore and "going at terrific speed". What he described as an illuminated saucer was seen last night by William Humphrey, 3148 S. 20th Street, he said. It was zigzagging directly over the Heil Co. plant, said Humphrey, and seemed to land in a wooded area nearby.

[*Alamo Register*, July 1947]

CUERO RESIDENTS SEE FLYING DISC

Cuero has finally produced its first flying disc. It was reported by Mrs Haak of 410 Stockdale Street, and her husband. However, Mrs Haak's disc is no particular mystery to her. She thinks she knows what caused it. It was simply a reflection of an airplane, she said.

[*Alamo Times*, July 1947]

FIRST IT'S FLYING DISKS — NOW IT'S "FIRE BALLS" PEOPLE SEE

A lot of Texans are "disk-gusted" with the flying saucers, but others are just plain "disk-turbed".

Flying balls of fire circled a wide area around Palestine and some negroes, believing the end of the world was near, began praying. A white man grabbed a rifle and shot at the mysterious objects. Sheriff Paul Stanford of Anderson County described them as orange basketballs of fire.

- It was the first time the aerial objects were reported in that area. Residents of the Brushy Greek community, 15 miles northeast of Palestine, called Sheriff Stanford about 8.30 last night, saying 12 balls were flying in a straight line over the community. Then, they reported, the balls formed a circle which began moving toward Palestine.

By 9 pm hundreds of Palestine spectators reported seeing as many as three balls in the sky at once, moving in a circle. Sheriff Stanford discounted any suggestion that the balls originated from a spotlight.

Bud Everett, druggist, chased them for a better view. He said they finally disappeared about 11 pm. Mrs Horace Valentine said she saw two perfectly round balls that "nearly scared me to death" when they appeared over her home.

JULY, 1947: CORRESPONDENCE

To FBI, Washington DC

Gentlemen,   July 6, 1947
For your information and for whatever value it
may be I should like to report seeing one of the
"flying discs" on July 4. It appeared to have started
from the dance hall here at Asbury Park and
momentarily I thought it was a balloon but it went
in a definite direction at an apparently constant
speed and gradually ascending following a path
similar to the trajectory of a bullet but more pro-
nounced. It disappeared in the distance going north

along the shore line. Glenn Miller and Tex Benechi were presently at the dance hall.

I hope this may be of some help to you.

(X)
Asbury Park
Jersey City

Teletype to Director FBI

From: FBI New Orleans   July 7, 1947
Very urgent: Flying discs, miscellaneous
(X) of Shreveport, Louisiana, advises he observed a circular disc at 6.05 pm this date coming from NW direction. Disc landed in 1500 block of Texas Avenue. (X) picked up disc at 1554 Texas Avenue. Disc whirling when seen in air and fire seen spouting from sides. Fire went out on landing and smoke issued few seconds after fire went out. Disc picked up and not hot. (X) notified G-2 Barksdale immediately and they took disc before SA [Special Agent] arrived.

Disc description: thin aluminium disc 16″ in diameter. Has small coils 2″ in diameter and 4″ long at the ends of the diameter. Coils connected by two copper wires to two terminals on each coil and these wires are connected at the crossing in the center of each disc to an object 1″ in diameter by 2″ long, similar to starter on fluorescent light. Center object has on upper end: "Made in USA".

Made sound like a policeman's whistle and smooth side toward earth in flight. Barksdale Field agreed if not [harmful] would turn over to FBI if we want it subject to superior instructions. Names of all persons who handled disc before arrival of agent secured. Barksdale Field making photos. Will secure and forward photos to Bureau. Believed press aware of incident.

FBI New Orleans

Office memorandum of the US Government to
Mr D. M. Ladd

From: H. B. Fletcher   July 7, 1947

At 10.45 am, July 7, 1947, I talked to SAC Johnson of the Milwaukee Office concerning the United Press item appearing in the *Washington Post* for Monday, July 7, with reference to a flying disc or flying saucer allegedly reported to the Milwaukee Office by Reverend Joseph Brasky of St Joseph's Church, Grafton, Wisconsin.

SAC Johnson advised that the Associated Press and the United Press between the hours 1.00 and 6.00 am today had made inquiry of him as to whether anything had been reported to the Milwaukee Office. He declined to comment. He stated as a matter of fact the priest had not made any contact with him, and he learned from the Associated Press that the priest was intoxicated and as far as the Associated Press was concerned they were not releasing the story because all that was involved was a circular saw. Mr Johnson stated the *Milwaukee Sentinel* apparently sent the report out and that they handled United Press service. He stated a photograph of the priest was in this morning's paper holding a circular saw which apparently covers the body of the priest from arm pit to arm pit. Attached to the saw are several wires and two small tubes described as about 3″ long and 1″ in diameter. The news item in the *Milwaukee Sentinel* indicates it was believed some prankster had thrown it into the yard, perhaps with a firecracker attached. Mr Johnson stated the *Milwaukee Sentinel* had stated the priest would make a report of this matter today to the Milwaukee Office. I instructed SAC Johnson, in the event the priest made a report, to furnish details of the report immediately, but in view of the nature of the information in his possession, no inquiry should be conducted at the present.

Telegram to FBI, Washington DC

7.14 pm, July 7, 1947
Check files in inventors' council for drawing of multi-spring catapult. This invention sent by me to War Department in 1945. Possible leakage of information has resulted. My device or variation

therefrom could conceivably catapult a disc and in silence for several miles.

(X),
San Marcos, Texas

Teletype to Director and SAC, Cincinnati

From: FBI Dallas   6.17 pm, July 8, 1947
Urgent: Flying disc, information concerning.
(X), Headquarters Eighth Air Force, telephonically advised this office that an object purporting to be a flying disc was recovered near Roswell, New Mexico, this date. The disc is hexagonal in shape and was suspended from a balloon by cable, which balloon was approximately 20 feet in diameter. (X) further advised that the object found resembles a high altitude weather balloon with a radar reflector, but that telephonic conversation between their office and Wright Field had not borne out this belief. Disc and balloon being transported to Wright Field by special plane for examination. Information provided this office because of national interest in case and fact that National Broadcasting Company, Associated Press, and others attempting to break story of location of disc today. Advised would request Wright Field to advise Cincinnati office results of examination. No further investigation being conducted.

FBI Dallas

Office memorandum of the US Government to Director FBI

From: SAC, Milwaukee   July 8, 1947
Subject: Flying discs or saucers: miscellaneous —
telephone call from Mr Fletcher at the Bureau at
8.30 am, July 7, 1947.

Attached are newspaper clippings from the
Milwaukee Sentinel and *Milwaukee Journal* of July 7,
1947 [see newspaper extracts for July].

For the Bureau's information, United Press and
Associated Press telephoned me at my residence
about three or four times between 1.00 am and
2.30 am, July 7, 1947. The United Press representative informed me that Father Joseph Brasky had
stated on interview by a *Milwaukee Sentinel*
reporter, one Bill Weeks, that he, Father Brasky, was
going to call the FBI concerning the contraption,
which apparently was identical with one of the flying discs recently publicized throughout the
country. The United Press representative desired to
know if we had any statement to make on the matter. I informed him that I had no official comment,
other than "no comment".

Since I have contacted the United Press representative on various occasions, I asked him what
the actual details were, and he stated he did not
know except that the interview of the priest
reflected that a circular saw had been found with
some devices attached to it.

The Associated Press called me shortly after the United Press representative did, and was advised that I had no comment to make concerning the story. I asked the Associated Press representative what the actual facts were, and he informed me that as far as the Associated Press was concerned, the facts were that a circular saw had been found and a story had been obtained from a priest who had been drinking quite heavily. The Associated Press representative informed me that apparently the United Press desired to get a statement from me denying or affirming that the FBI was investigating the matter. I informed the Associated Press representative that apparently someone was suffering under a misinterpretation of any comment I had made, and possibly some reporter was in an embarrassing position if a story had gone out over the wire services.

I then telephoned the United Press representative, who apparently in the meantime had been called by the Associated Press in an effort to straighten out the United Press. No reference was made to the FBI in the *Milwaukee Sentinel* article appearing July 7, 1947, but the *Milwaukee Journal* article [see p.23] referred to an alleged statement by Father Brasky that he attempted to get in touch with an FBI agent whom he knows. Father Brasky has never contacted the Milwaukee FBI Office or any agent concerning his find. In my opinion, this is just another hoax story, since a photograph of

Father Brasky with the saw indicates no basis for any investigation by any authority.

To FBI, Washington DC

Dear FBI,   July 8, 1947
It is my opinion about those "flying discs" reported seen over Kentucky, New Mexico, California, Oregon, Washington, Idaho, Colorado, South Carolina and Eastern Canada that some European country is using them by filling them up with germs or explosives, and after a couple thousand miles they drop their contents and disappear.

Also I suggest that you keep lots of disinfectant on hand. Or else something might happen to us in the United States.

FROM A FRIEND

To J. Edgar Hoover, Washington DC

Dear Mr Hoover,   July 9, 1947
I have also seen a flying saucer — the evening of July 4 — about 10.30 pm — only it was in the air at the same level as two obvious portions of light in the searchlight beams from the air field at Lake St Clair. I was sitting on my porch at the time. A few trucks could with proper equipment create the same illusion. There were two clearly outlined

beams — one partly faded out. The saucer appeared when the third beam faded out from the ground to the saucer. Recently I mentioned the distressed ship in the Pacific not being due entirely to natural phenomena, and coordinating that ship, the bomb disaster soon after that, the stab murder case — the recent Manila story — are the "flying saucers" army or vigilante?

I am still American only! Believe that our age is predestined — but that we must all play our parts in this age, and maybe it was my work to glance up from my porch July 4th — to an illusion — not delusion — saucer!

Again this will be unsigned.

Office memorandum of the US Government to D. M. Ladd

From: J.P. Coyne   July 10, 1947
Subject: (X), informant
There is being attached hereto a Western Union telegram received from the above individual in which information is furnished concerning a "disc". This telegram has been acknowledged.

Action:
It is recommended that this telegram be turned over to the Liaison Section in order that they may make the information contained therein available to the War Department.

Telegram to US Dept of Justice, Washington DC

6.30 pm, July 6, 1947

About 12 so-called flying discs passed over Darlington, South Carolina approximately 5.30 pm today. Advise if wish details.

(X)

Office memorandum of the US Government to
D.M. Ladd

From: (X)   July 11, 1947
Subject: Flying discs
SAC Bannister of the Butte Office called at noon today and stated that (X) of Twin Falls, Idaho, at 2.45 am Mountain Time today heard a noise in the back of her home. She thought a collision had occurred and investigated and found in the back yard of the home next door an object described as follows:

A disc 30½″ in diameter, circular in shape, it is dished like a saucer and actually there is a saucer within a saucer in the manner of cymbals. On one surface there is attached a plastic dome described as about 14″ in diameter and affixed by 8 bolts in a rather rough manner. The bolts can best be described as similar to stove bolts. On the other surface is another dome of metal which is gold in color on one side and on the inside is silver in color, which looks like tin. Through the plastic dome can be observed three tubes similar to radio tubes and there is some wiring. The disc generally is 10″ thick and at the point where the domes are located about 14″ in thickness. There is an object on it similar to electric coil which has some type of an arm on it and bears the words "Inspected TS". Some of the wiring has been burned off and it looks as though something might be missing.

(X) stated that if this were the work of some prankster he went to quite a bit of trouble. He stated the press is aware of this incident. He stated that the disc had been picked up and was now at the Police Department, Twin Falls, Idaho. He was instructed to notify the local Army authorities of the existence of this disc.

Office memorandum of the US Government to (X)

From: (X)   July 11, 1947
Subject: Flying disc
At 10.45 pm on the evening of July 11, 1947, Clerk (X) of the Washington Field Office called and stated that at the instruction of Mr Hennrich he wanted to pass on to the Bureau information he had just received from (X) of Laurel, Maryland, to the effect that a "flying disc" had just landed in (X)'s yard "and the machinery is still buzzing." The clerk stated (X) was apparently so excited he had a

difficult time even getting his name out, and no further detail could be obtained from him.

At 10.50 pm I passed the above information on to the duty officer at G–2 who indicated he had also received the same data from another source, and would pass our information along to appropriate Army quarters.

(X) of the Associated Press called at about 10.55 pm and asked whether the Bureau had received any report on a "flying disc" in Laurel, Maryland. After checking with Mr Nichols I told him we had received such a report and had passed it on to Army authorities.

Office memorandum of the US Government to
Mr E.A. Tamm

From: D. M. Ladd   July 11, 1947
SAC Johnson of the Milwaukee Office called to advise he had just received a telephone call from Colonel (X), Reserve Officer with the Civilian Air Patrol, Black River Falls, Wisconsin. Colonel (X) reported that at 3.30 pm, July 10, (X) at Black River Falls, Wisconsin, had found a large 17″ disc which appeared to have been possibly made out of cardboard painted with silver airplane dope [lubricant]. In the center was a tube and a small motor with a propeller attached to the side. Colonel (X) expressed the opinion that this disc would not be

able to fly by itself. He advised it would be taken to the Air Corps Headquarters. Colonel (X) advised, however, that (X) did not want to release the disc without FBI approval.

I instructed Mr Johnson to advise the Air Corps officer to get in touch with Colonel (X) and tell him he saw no reason for the Bureau to attempt to secure the release of the material since it was not in our custody and we had no control. He stated the press was also calling concerning this matter. I instructed him to make no comment to the press.

Office memorandum of the US Government to
Mr D.M. Ladd

From: (X)   July 12, 1947
Subject: Flying discs
Reference is made to (X)'s memorandum to you dated July 11, in the above-captioned matter.

At 11.55 pm, July 11, I took a phone call from (X) of the Laurel, Maryland, Police Department. Sergeant (X) said that he had examined the "flying disc". He said that it had been made from a Gulf Oil sign and the top of a garbage can and had been painted with aluminum paint. It had been recently painted because the paint was still wet. Attached to it were a dry cell battery, a flashlight bulb, some wires and a buzzer. He asked if the Bureau was sending anyone out to look at it. Told him that we were not, that we had referred the matter to the Army, and suggested that he call them.

I subsequently telephoned the duty officer at G-2, and passed on to him the information furnished by Sergeant Lonis.

To J. Edgar Hoover, Director, FBI

Dear Sir,   July 11, 1947
Have you seen one of the mysterious "saucers"?

What did it look like?

Do you think these strange, celestial manifestations are harbingers of a better day?

Do you believe it means that a new and revolutionary advance is coming?

Will it make your life brighter, happier, more useful?

We believe one of these startling discs is on its way to you. Then the secret will be out.

THE COMBINED AND AMALGAMATED COMMITTEE OF SKY-SCANNERS, DISC DECIPHERS and NEW-PRODUCT INTRODUCERS

To the FBI, Washington DC

Gentlemen,   July 12, 1947
I do send to you something new from Texas. Flying
[object] of fire circled around the Palestine and the
people are afraid of it. And around Cuero, not far
away from Yoakum, fell down some kind of light
from an airplane. Anyway got in their hands enemy
or Nazi mob and [they] want to ruin Texas.

They did start in Texas City demolish the fac-
tory. In the private part of Yoakum airport and
broadcasting station are such aliens my like that we
do not know who [they are]. Now got no airplanes
here, just hangars and broadcasting tower with lights
on rolling towers, and lights are like needles to our
eyes.

And got the light around the whole airport and
from the lights is running the electric and makes us
sick. And the air is full of electric by lightning in
some fireball from [the] telephone box in the store,
far away above half mile.

The airport is connected with *Alamo Register* in
San Antonio and people are talking with us. The
people are Archbishop Robert Lucy, living in new
residence and talking with us in the broadcasting
station and *Alamo Register* press, and with the old
archbishop's residence, and with the Cathedral
priests.

The Alamo Broadcasting is operated by two German old men, and they are now sick from the electric and they talk with us, and there are two men more and they are fighting together and we can hear them.

The archbishop is a bad man and working nothing. All work is done by the Cathedral Board. In the old archbishop's residence are some priests. One is named Morkovsky, he is a bad man too. He was in a car wreck with archbishop's car and his mother is killed and from that time he is living in the old residence, and talking with us. His brother is a priest in Hallettesville and is talking with us too.

All the people live something like trash, are not citizens of the United States, do not speak English, they say they are coming from Czechoslovakia. The Cathedral Board men and priests are German and they all are working for Germany. See such strange people we got in Texas and the Alamo place, that is saint to Texas people, fighting against the Mexicans' Santa Ana.

And I am ending with words: remember Alamo and Texas City.

Mrs (X), Mr (X)
Yoakum, Texas

To J. Edgar Hoover, FBI, Washington DC

Dear Mr Hoover,   July 14, 1947

In today's paper I see more news concerning the flying saucers. Now those are without a doubt from Russia, see they are likely checking how completely they can cover the US in one shot. I feel it is wrong for us to report areas in which they are seen.

In traveling I sat by a spiritualist and wasn't sure what she was. I talked to obtain as much information as I could. I became interested when she said, "Russia has a poison which they will place in an atom bomb that will destroy not one city but dozens of cities," so when I read of the flying saucers I wonder if Russia hasn't perfected a device which might destroy our whole country in one shot — I see that flying saucers were reported in Michigan, Illinois, New Orleans. These harmless discs were sent out to determine what area they cover — we are foolish to give them total information.

Now this woman may only be guessing but it should not be passed up. The name she gave me was (X) of Milwaukee, Wisconsin.

Why do we wait till we are destroyed or nearly so before we act? If we aren't ready in three seconds the next war will end all. I seem to see it all clearly in these latest events.

Let our War Department take notice — it's no time to sleep. We should secretly draft men, have all our guns set for a moment's notice.

We must be ready. But can we afford to wait if Russia plans destroying us in one shot? Why not let her have it and have it in big doses first. That's the only way I can see us having end of it at all.

(X)
Woodstock, Illinois

To FBI, Washington DC

Ha! Ha! Winchell has revealed the "Saucer" secret. You can't hide anything from us and our agents like Winchell.

COMMUNIST
[Anonymous note, date stamped July 16, 1947]

AUGUST, 1947

Memorandum to Director of Intelligence,
War Department General Staff, The Pentagon,
Washington DC. Attention: Colonel L. R. Forney,
Chief, Security Group

From: John Edgar Hoover, Director FBI
Subject: (X)   August 5, 1947
There are attached hereto copies of a letter received
from the above-captioned individual, together with
copies of a newspaper clipping enclosure, concerning "flying discs".

(X)'s letter has been acknowledged and he has been advised that copies of his letter have been furnished to you for your consideration.

To FBI, Washington DC

Gentlemen,

On July 7, 1947, 10.30 pm my mother-in-law and I witnessed a flaming object which dropped in street in front of our house at (X), Nebraska.

Upon examination, the object was solid and had form of round circular disc, approximately the size of a silver dollar and ¼" thick, burning with intense heat. The *World Herald* newspaper was notified and reporter was sent out.

In the meantime, a boy picked up the object and it fell in pieces. When the reporter arrived he scooped up the fragments and said he would have them analyzed. Your attention is directed to attached analysis.

There were six people who actually saw the object and can testify to the extreme heat at which it was burning. We did not claim it was one of the so-called "flying saucers" or any such phenomena but we did want some kind of reasonable explanation because if this object had dropped on a roof top it would have certainly set fire. We can definitely say it was not tobacco ashes as was expressed by (X). It burned with such extreme heat as to scorch pavement on and near pavement where it lit.

This could have been a late Fourth of July firework or something similar but at any rate we are calling it to your attention, as the answer the "learned" doctor gave as pipe ashes is full of ridicule and entirely unsatisfactory.

(X)

[*Source unknown*]

"FLYING SAUCER" JUST SOMEONE'S PIPE DREAM

The "flying saucer" that fell near 2319 Himebaugh Avenue Monday evening was nothing but "ashes from somebody's pipe dream."

So says Dr C. L. Kenny, head of the chemistry department at the Creighton College of Dentistry. He had two students analyze the ashes. They found sodium, potassium, iron, aluminium, carbonate, sulphate and unburnt carbon, he said. "This is the same analysis you would get from ordinary pipe tobacco," Dr Kenny said.

Teletype to Director FBI

Urgent   August 7, 1947
Flying object reported over Philadelphia, August 6, 1947. Sabotage. *The Philadelphia Inquirer* on August 7, 1947 carried item concerning flying objects

observed over Philadelphia on evening of August 6, 1947. People reported as observing such interviewed by Philadelphia Office, and substantially furnished following information. At 10.45, August 6, 1947, a bluish, white flaming object was observed at a height of 1,000 feet or more over Philadelphia proceeding from a northeasterly to a southwesterly direction. This object left a trail of smoke, which lasted for about 2 seconds, and a hissing or buzzing sound was audible after the sight of such object. People observing the same seemed responsible and reliable, and include a former Army air corps pilot. He does not believe above-mentioned object was a jet-propelled plane since the accompanying sound was not as loud as that made by jet-propelled planes. He estimated above object traveled at a rate of about 400 to 500 mph. Inquiries being made by Army and Navy Intelligence forces, Philadelphia on the request of the Philadelphia Office to determine if either Army or Navy are doing experimental work on new types of planes in vicinity of Philadelphia. They will advise Philadelphia Office in next several days. Letter of details will follow.

BOARDMAN
FBI Philadelphia

Teletype to Director FBI

5.21 pm, August 14, 1947

Urgent: L.R. Brummett, Sid Decker, flying discs, internal security

Seattle Post Intelligencer published article to effect that L. R. Brummett, Box 254, Redmond, Washington and Sidney Decker, Box 296, Redmond, Washington had sighted two discs at approximately 9 am August 13, 1947. Upon interview Decker stated that two very bright objects traveling at an extreme rate of speed were noticed by him as he was standing near the Redmond Post Office. Decker described the objects as having no wings, no tail and both ends were tapered. Decker added that the objects resembled a belly tank and that they were noiseless. The objects were very bright and traveling in a northeasterly direction over Redmond, Washington, one a bit behind and a little above the other, maintaining equal rates of speed for approximately 8 seconds at which time they disappeared from view. Decker added that they were higher than a plane generally travels. Brummett advised that he noticed the objects and called Decker's attention to them and also pointed them out to a Mrs Mamie English. Brummett stated that he saw two objects flying at a 45-degree angle northeasterly over Redmond and traveling at least three times faster than a plane. Brummett added that he watched the objects from 5 to 8 seconds at which time they disappeared from sight. According to Brummett the objects were described as being noiseless, having no wings or tail, lighter than aluminium, tapered at both ends and one stayed a little behind and a bit above the other and both maintained equal rates of speed. From Brummett's observation he was unable to decide whether the objects were flat or round. Mrs Mamie English stated that when Brummett called her attention to the objects she took a passing glance at the sky and could offer no description other than they looked like two silver balls traveling at a fast rate of speed.

WILCOX
FBI Seattle

Teletype to Director FBI

August 14, 1947

Bruce Armstrong, M. A. Nichols: flying discs internal security

Newspaper *Seattle Post Intelligencer* carried article on August 12 of report of flying discs seen by one Bruce Armstrong of Boeing Aircraft Company, and M. A. Nichols, 1125, South West 102nd Street, Seattle. Investigation of sighting by Armstrong reveals object to have been piece of paper, which had been seen by control tower at Boeing Field. Investigation of sighting by

M. A. Nichols indicates object was a weather balloon. Letter to follow.

WILCOX
FBI Seattle

Teletype to Director FBI

August 15, 1947

Flying disks — Security Matter X
A Mr (X) of Agate Beach, near Ocean Lake, Oregon has reported that on the evening of August 7 at 11.30 pm, he sighted what he believed to be a disc bright in color which he was able to observe for only a short time because of its speed. Bartlett to be interviewed.

BOBBITT
FBI Portland

Teletype to Director, FBI

Urgent: Flying discs   August 15, 1947
On instant date, (X) of Twin Falls, Idaho, and (X), Idaho, same community, advised that on Wednesday morning, August 13 last, at approximately 9.30 am while fishing in river approximately 40 miles south-west of Twin Falls, Idaho, in isolated country they saw two objects flying through the air at great height, which appeared to be discs, and at same time heard roar similar to noise created by motor truck. Informants advised objects moving very rapidly and

that they each appeared to be approximately 6 feet in diameter. Objects quickly disappeared from sight and have not been seen since. No further description of these objects presently available. Further investigation being conducted by this division pursuant to Bureau Bulletin No. 42, Sub Division B, dated July 30, 1947. Bureau will be promptly informed of all pertinent developments.

BANISTER
FBI Butte

Office memorandum of the US government to
D. M. Ladd

From: (X)   August 20, 1947
There is attached hereto copies of two memoranda dated July 24, 1947, and July 16, 1947 [not included], concerning (X) of Dallas, Texas, (X) of Oklahoma City, Oklahoma, and (X). These memoranda were made available to Special Agent (X) of the Liaison Section by General Schulgen of the Army Air Forces Intelligence.

General Schulgen requested that the Bureau conduct a background investigation of these two individuals mentioned in the attached memoranda since they were among the first to sight the alleged flying discs. He indicated that he desired that the investigation be directed toward ascertaining whether or not either of these individuals have any subversive background and to ascertain

whether or not they had any ulterior motive for
reporting these sightings.

Recommendation:
It is recommended this memorandum be forwarded to the Internal Security Section.

*Memorandum to the Security Officer, Ocama,
Tinker Field*

July 24, 1947

From: Kaiman D. Simon, CI, US Army
Subject: (X), Radio Corporation of America, Dallas,
Texas; residence (X), Oklahoma City, Oklahoma:
flying discs
On July 23, 1947, (X) was interviewed at his resi-
dence in Oklahoma City, Oklahoma, relating to his
alleged viewing of a flying disc over the vicinity of
Oklahoma City, Oklahoma.

Subject, whose age is 38, advised that he is
married and has one child and is presently the
holder of a Private Pilot's License. Subject averred
he has extensively studied electronics, sound engi-
neering and aeronautics, and his present occu-
pation is (X) for Radio Corporation of America,
offices of which are located in Dallas, Texas. (X)
stated that between the days 17 May to 21 May
1947, just after dusk he observed an object which
he believed to be a small aircraft in the south. He
advised that the sun had just gone down and the

moon had not yet arisen on the horizon. Savage related that he and his wife had just departed their residence and had started to enter their car in the driveway. He judged the time to be between 8.30 pm and 9.00 pm, and the lights from the city of Oklahoma City appeared to be shining on this object when he first saw it. He judged the object to be about 160 degrees in the south when he first saw it, and as it moved toward him he remarked to his wife that "a big white plane was coming over".

(X) stated that when this object was at a 45 degree angle from him, he realized it was not a conventional type aircraft, and it appeared elliptical at first and as it moved closer it appeared perfectly round and was flat. He advised the object, which appeared to him as a disc, had no appearance of being spherical and had a ratio of diameter to the thickness of approximately 10 to 1, appearing thicker in the center, but this could not be positively ascertained. He judged the object to be at an altitude of between 10,000 and 18,000 feet, and it left no trailing effects. He related that it appeared to be in bulk as big as the bulk of six B–29s at an altitude of approximately the same height. He advised that the object was in his vision approximately 15 to 20 seconds and traveled at a speed which he judged to be approximately three times that of jet–propelled aircraft.

(X) stated that there were no protrusions on this object and as it went by he listened for a sound of noise, and at one time thought he distinguished a swishing sound like the rushing of air. This swishing sound occurred a few seconds after this object had passed him. He averred this sound was not very loud and did not last very long, and it is very possible that the sound could have been his imagination or expectation, as he was not sure of the sound. He related that he called his wife to see the object, but it had disappeared before she could focus her eyes on it. Subject stated that the object appeared to diminish in size and speed as it moved away, and it was moving in a direction of 350 degrees to the north. Subject further stated that the object appeared to be frosty white in colour at all times.

(X) advised that he has held a pilot's certificate since 1934 and has been flying since 1929. He advised that he would be glad to answer any further inquiries and will cooperate in every way possible. He stated he was sure this object was not a meteor and in his opinion it must be radically built and powered, probably atomic.

Office memorandum of the US Government to Director FBI

From: SAC, Butte   August 20, 1947
Subject: Flying disks; refer teletype to Bureau dated August 15, 1947
Enclosed please find the newspaper account carried by the *Twin Falls, Idaho Times News* on August 15,

together with a sheet of paper on which A.C. Urie attempted to sketch his impressions of the instrument which he claims to have seen [not included].

Concerning Urie's sketches, it may be noted that he believed the rolled outer edge, which he attempted to create in his drawing, to have been about a foot through. Urie likewise believed that the tubing or exhaust flame, which he and his sons claim to have seen, was about a foot through and extended at least to the back end of the device. The flame did not appear to taper off or to widen out toward the back.

Billy and Keith Urie stated that they could see a knot on the side of the device from which the flames were shooting, and that they could see daylight between the exhaust flame and the side of the device. The flames did not leave any smoke or odor.

The Urie boys thought that the "side view" sketch should show that the device was more sharply angled from bottom to top, while Urie himself thought that it was more streamlined and curved. Urie said that the instrument came to a pointed or rounded top.

In his notations, Urie mistakenly said that he had seen it on Thursday. During interview, he stated that it had actually been on Wednesday, August 13, 1947, when he and his sons saw the contrivance about 1.00 pm.

Urie explained that he had sent his boys to the river to get some rope from his boat. When he thought they were overdue, he went outside his tool shed to look for them. He noticed them about 300 feet away looking in the sky and he glanced up to see what he called the flying disc. He said he could only see it for a moment before it disappeared behind a hill that obscured his view.

Urie further stated that the contrivance was about 75 feet in the air. Urie resides in the depths of the Snake River Canyon, which is about 400 feet deep and 1,200 feet across at that place. According to his account, the contrivance was about 300 feet below the rim of the canyon and he saw it against the steep walls of the canyon on the far side. He described its color as sky-blue and stated that he doubted if it could be seen against the sky. He likewise said that it was purely by chance that he saw it. It did not spin like a top.

As the machine went by the Urie place, the trees over which it almost directly passed (Mormon poplars) did not just bend with the wind as if a plane had gone by, but, in Urie's words, "spun around on top as if they were in a vacuum".

Keith Urie, 8 years of age, said he first saw the machine coming down the canyon, heading from east to west and following the contours of the ground. Billy, aged 10, saw it almost immediately. Both watched it fly out of sight behind a tree in a matter of moments. They said that they then ran to their father and learned that he too had seen the machine.

Urie seemed completely sincere about the incident. He said his wife and daughter were in the house at the time and had not seen the machine. He questioned his brother, who also lives in the canyon, but his brother had been eating at the time and had seen nothing. Urie and his two boys maintained that they had never before seen one of the discs. Urie, when interviewed, appeared to be a sober, middle-aged man.

(X), who originally furnished Special Agents with information about the incident, likewise stated that Urie appeared completely sincere about the machine.

No further attempt was made to locate L. W. Hawkins, inasmuch as (X), who was with Hawkins at the time, was interviewed. (X)'s name was withheld from the newspaper because Hawkins and (X) were fishing at Salmon Dam while (X) was supposed to have been working at Twin Falls.

(X) said simply that he and Hawkins could hear a roar. They looked up and could see two instruments flying at a great height, which (X) mentioned might have been between 4,000 and 6,000 feet. However, he said he had no idea how large the devices were and consequently, they may have been several miles away. He said that that he and Hawkins were satisfied they had seen something and they were very doubtful that they had seen two planes.

[*Twin Falls Times-News,* August 15, 1947]

FLYING SAUCER REPORTED
FLASHING DOWN CANYON AT 1,000
MPH; TWO OTHERS ARE SEEN

Just as Magic Valley and the nation were starting to let go of lampposts after reeling under a welter of flying saucer reports, two more Twin Falls county men revived speculation on the mystery with vivid descriptions of discs they saw.

From A. C. Urie, who operates the Auger Falls Trout Farm 6 miles west of Blue Lakes ranch in Snake River Canyon, came perhaps the most detailed account of one of the fast-flying objects the nation has yet produced.

The flying saucer Urie saw was skimming along through Snake River Canyon at a height of about 75 feet at 1 pm Wednesday. At 9.30 am the same day, L. W. Hawkins, Twin Falls county commissioner and former county sheriff (X) also saw two circular objects moving along at a great height, near Salmon Dam 40 miles north east of Twin Falls.

Here is Urie's eyewitness description of the flying discs seen by him and his sons, Keith, 8, and Billy, 10:

> I obtained a close-up view of the flying saucer as
> it passed by the trout farm at 1 pm August 13
> going down Snake River Canyon at a height of

> about 75 feet from the canyon floor. I would
> estimate the speed at about 1,000 miles per hour.

Urie explained that the incident occurred while the two boys were coming across the river from the north side in a boat. He had become concerned about what was delaying them, and had walked down toward the river to see if they were all right.

> I had a side view at a distance of about 300 feet
> and almost about level with the thing. Two of my
> boys, Keith and Billy, were below me and they also
> saw it at about a similar angle. They both got a
> side view, and we were all looking at it from the
> south side of the river facing towards the north.
> The boys saw it coming about half a mile up the
> canyon, and we all lost sight of it in less than a
> mile.
>
> It rode up and down over the hills and hollows
> at a speed indicating some type of control faster
> than the reflexes of man. It is my opinion that it
> is guided by instruments and must be powered by
> atomic energy, as it made very little noise—just a
> swish as it passed by.

Urie described the size as about 20 feet long by 10 feet high and 10 feet wide, giving it an oblong shape. It might be described as looking like an inverted pie plate or broad-brimmed straw hat that had been compressed from two sides.

Pressed for his candid opinion of just what it was, Urie said that he was convinced that there was something to this flying saucer situation.

> I know a number of people who have also seen them and I know that they're not just imagining something or trying to get their names in the paper. I do know that it scared the boys and made me feel pretty uneasy.

Tracing down a rumor that County Commissioner Hawkins had seen an unusual object in the air on the same day as Urie's experience, the *Times-News* called him at his Piler home. "Yes, I did," he replied without hesitation. "I'll have to admit I've been sceptical all along until I saw it with my own eyes. I can't say what it was, but I can say there's something in the air."

Hawkins related that while at Salmon Dam Wednesday morning, a sound resembling the echo of a motor caused him to look upward, and there he saw two circular objects that reflected light. They were traveling at a great speed and higher than most airplanes, according to Hawkins.

Aside from this, he declined to add details except to say, "There's something in the air."

To Commanding Officer, Army Air Forces,
Washington, DC. Attn: Lt Col George Garrett

Subject: Flying saucer   August 25, 1947

1. The specimens of an alleged "flying saucer" brought to this Command by Colonel H. M. McCoy, which were obtained by the FBI and given to Lt Col Garrett, were examined to determine their connection, if any, with the so-called "flying saucers", or any project at HQ, AMC, Wright Field. The specimens were carefully examined by both technicians of the Analysis Division (T-2) and Electronics Sub-division (T-3). The latter organization stated that these specimens definitely had no connection whatsoever with the "Mogul" project nor with any other research and development project of this Command.

2. It is also the opinion of this Command that these specimens have no connection with the so-called "Flying saucer" or "Disc". These specimens, therefore, are considered as part of a hoax that could be perpetrated by most anyone seeking publicity or for any other reasons.

3. The specimens include fragments of an undeterminable shape made from plaster of Paris or similar ceramic and containing some electrical resistance wire for measurement or heating purposes. The condition of the ceramic indicates that the resistance wire was heated electrically at

one time or another. The fragments could not be connected with any AMC project. The other articles are identified as follows:

(a) An outmoded type of magnetic speaker diaphragm made of aluminium alloy, manufactured by the Nathaniel Baldwin Company of Salt Lake City, Utah, which was first patented May 1, 1910. This article cannot be connected with any AMC project.

(b) The second and third articles are Bakelite coil forms wrapped with ordinary thin enamel copper wire. These coils indicate that they were skillfully made at one time but were crudely rewrapped by one not familiar with the art of making a coil. These coils also have no connection with any AMC project.

(c) The fourth article is a metallic box which is the remains of an electronic filter condenser made by the Polymet manufacturing company of New York, New York. This article also has no connection with any AMC project.

(d) The fifth article is the remains of a metallic magnetic ring that could not be identified as any part of any device used at this command.

4. This information may be transmitted to the FBI to inform various agencies throughout the

United States as to what action to take in the event other similar specimens are found.

H. M. McCoy
Colonel, Air Corps
Deputy Commanding General
Intelligence (T-2)

Office memorandum of the US Government to Director FBI. Attention: Assistant Director D. M. Ladd

From: SAC, San Francisco   August 27, 1947
Subject: Reports of flying discs
Colonel (X), Fourth Air Force, Hamilton Field, California, telephonically advised Special Agent (X) of the San Francisco Office at 10.40 am on August 27, 1947, that a personal letter had been received by his organization from (X), city editor of the *Seattle Times*, which stated in effect that because there were so many stories going around relative to flying discs and related matters, and that his staff of reporters had been attempting to get reliable information concerning such stories, he was writing to inquire whether any governmental agency was going to make an official statement relative to the situation pertaining to the flying discs; that the editor also asks whether it would be permissible for his reporters to interview the Special Agent relative to the situation.

Colonel (X) stated that the above-mentioned letter was answered personally by General (X) on

August 25, 1947, and advised the *Seattle Times* city editor that as far as the Army Air Force was concerned, they had no information which would definitely clear up the situation; that as far as interviewing persons, he could feel free to interview whomsoever he desired, in that there was no censorship at the present time; that in the interest of economy, the Fourth Air Force headquarters would not run out every lead or report of flying discs, but that if well-founded and apparently reliable information were received, that such information would be given attention.

A copy of this letter is being forwarded to the Seattle Field Division for any action deemed advisable.

Office memorandum of the US Government to Director FBI. Attention: Assistant Director D. M. Ladd

From: SAC, San Francisco   August 27, 1947
Subject: Reports of flying discs
In order to keep the Bureau fully informed, I am enclosing a letter dated July 28, 1947, entitled "Unidentified Objects", furnished to me by Lt Colonel (X), AC of SA-2. Enclosed with this letter was a memorandum for the officer in charge written by (X), Special Agent CIC ADC, dated July 15, 1947.

Lt Colonel (X) furnished me in person with a memorandum dated August 5, 1947, and prepared by (X), Special Agent CIC 4AF.

The Bureau will be kept currently advised of any future information obtained in this matter.

To Special Agent in Charge, FBI, San Francisco, California

Subject: "Unidentified objects"   July 28, 1947
Enclosed herewith is information copy of the memorandum for the officer in charge, subject as above, dated July 15, 1947.

DONALD L. SPRINGER
Headquarters Fourth Air Force
Office of the Assistant Chief of Staff
Intelligence (A–2)
Hamilton Field, California

Memorandum for the officer in charge

Unidentified objects   July 15, 1947
On July 14, 1947, (X) of 170th AAF Base Unit, Ferry Division, Brooks Field, San Antonio, Texas was interviewed and the following information was obtained:

(X) departed Williams Field, Arizona at 1400 CST on 28 June 1947 in a P-51 for Portland, Oregon. At approximately 1515 CST, on a course of 300 degrees and ground speed of 285, altitude 10,000 feet, approximately 30 miles northwest of Lake Meade, Nevada, (X) sighted five or six white, circular objects at four o'clock, altitude approximately 6,000 feet, course approximately 120 degrees and an estimated speed of 285 mph. (X) said the objects were flying very smoothly and in a close formation. The estimated size of the white objects was approximately 36″ in diameter. (X) stated that he is sure the white objects were not birds, since the rate of closure was very fast. Lt Armstrong was certain that the white objects were not jets or conventional-type aircraft since he has flown both types.

Agent's notes:
(X) was very sincere in the explanation and was not the exaggerating type. He merely stated what he saw and has drawn no conclusions as to what the white objects were.

LAWRENCE B. KING, Jr
Special Agent CIC ADF
Williams Field, Chandler, Arizona

Memorandum for the officer in charge

August 5, 1947

On August 5, 1947, this agent interviewed (X), the assistant operations officer in the 415th AAF Building, 96 Hamilton Field, California, regarding flying objects in the air. The officer stated in substance that on 29 July at 1450, he and a student, (X), Berkeley, California, landed and parked an airplane near the hangar building 69 of the 416th AA7–30. Walking from the aircraft toward reserve operations, and looking westward just over the hangar, (X) saw a P-80 flying southward toward Oakland. Above this P-80 at approximately 8,000 to 10,000 feet in altitude, (X) saw two flying objects traveling that same direction as the P-80. (X) judged the solid, white, somewhat shiny objects were approximately 15 to 25 feet in diameter. (X) stated that he didn't call them discs due to the publicity these objects have been given, but in shape they were circular, like a ball on the bottom, but not completely round, and (X) specifically stated that these objects were not airplanes.

The first flying object was traveling straight and level; whereas the second was close behind the first, same altitude, only it seemed to be going from left to right and right to left, more or less in an air-craft formation. (X) further stated that the speed of these two objects made a P-80 look as if it was motionless in the air. The sky was clear, consequently (X) watched the two objects until they disappeared in flight, supposedly over Oakland, headed toward the ocean. Due to the noise of the P-80, no sound of any kind could be heard from these flying objects. They did not leave any vapor, smoke, or any visible trails along their flight path.

(X) informed this agent he had never told anyone about these flying objects, fearing that people would think he was crazy.

Agent's notes:
(X) showed extreme sincerity throughout the interview, answering all questions with caution and assurance.

JAMES A. NELSON
Special Agent CIC 4AF

Office memorandum of the US Government to Director FBI

From: SAC, Butte   August 27, 1947
Subject: Flying discs sighted by (X), Tacoma, Washington — Security Matter X.
Re: Seattle tels August 7, 1947 and August 12, 1947, in the above-captioned matter.
(X), Mountain View Drive, Boise, Idaho, was inter-viewed at the Boise Resident Agency, Boise, Idaho, by SA (X), August 19, 1947. Mr (X) advised that he received a letter from (X) Editor of (X), Evanstown, Illinois, dated June 26, 1947, in which the editor advised that he was interested in publishing an article in his magazine concerning the flying discs seen by Mr (X) near Mount Rainier on June 24, 1947, which letter is being enclosed [see p. 92]. Mr (X) stated that he did not give much thought to the editor's letter until he wrote him again and informed him that (X) of Tacoma, Washington had sent him fragments of a flying disc and that he would like him to go to Tacoma, Washington, and contact (X) to see if there was any truth in their

story about the disc fragments. He stated that he did not answer the editor's letter, but inquired of several friends for their opinion in the matter, and that they all told him if (X) desired to pay his expenses to go to Tacoma, Washington, and look into this matter, that they did not see where he had anything to lose. He informed that he gave a talk at the Boise Ad Club on July 25, 1947, about the flying discs he had seen, and also of the request contained in the editor's letter to go to Tacoma to investigate additional information regarding the finding of disc fragments by (X) and (X).

Mr (X) advised that following his talk, he was approached by a person who said he knew both (X) and (X) and that they were very reliable individuals. He stated that after thinking it over, he called the editor by telephone and at which time he informed him that he would contact (X) and (X) and investigate the matter regarding the disc fragments, if the editor would send him $200 expense money. He also advised that he received $200 expense money from the editor by Western Union the next morning. He informed that he left for Tacoma, Washington, via his personal plane on July 30, 1947. Upon arriving at Pendleton, Oregon, he told his story to (X), CAA Inspector from Portland, Oregon, who advised him to go ahead with his investigation.

He stated that he landed at Barry's Airport in Tacoma and obtained a room at the Winthrop Hotel. He informed that he then called (X) by telephone to make arrangements to talk to him regarding the disc fragments. He advised that (X) insisted on coming to the hotel room immediately. Upon arriving at Mr (X)'s hotel room, (X) stated that he wanted him to forget about the discs as too many things had been happening to him, and advised Mr (X) to return home and forget about the discs. Mr (X) stated that he informed (X) that he wanted to obtain all of the information available regarding the disc fragments and that he understood that (X) had told the press about the disc fragments, stating that there was nothing to the story and that it was a phoney. (X) immediately replied that his story was not false or phoney, but that what he had seen and what had happened to him was so unusual and fantastic that he wanted to forget about the disc fragments. He then agreed to tell Mr (X) the following story, providing his name and the harbor patrols would be left out.

(X) stated that his dog had been killed and his boy hurt and that the wheel mount on his harbor patrol boat had been struck by disc fragments, and that about 20 tons of this material had fallen on the beach at Murray Island and into the bay, and that a day after the incident, a man about 40 years of age had contacted him and told him "I know what you saw at Murray Island and I'm telling you in a nice way to forget about it and keep your mouth shut." (X) stated that he obtained a large number of the fragments and had taken them home, but that his superior officer had told him to send some of the fragments to (X) at Chicago; that he would analyze the specimens free of charge. (X) continued stating that on the afternoon of June 21, 1947, he was on patrol with his boy, dog and two seamen near a cove on the east side of Murray Island. He stated that he looked up through the windshield of the boat and at a height of about 1,000 feet, he saw six round circular gray objects that looked like large inner tubes slightly squashed. These objects appeared to be about 100 feet across and in the center was a hole about 25 feet. (X) said he assumed they were some type of a balloon. The object in the center was lower than the rest of the other objects, and the other objects were circling around it. The object in the center seemed to be descending while the others followed. As the objects descended he saw portholes around the inside of the object and what appeared to be windows. He stated that the object in the center descended to about 500 feet, and that suddenly one of the circling objects came down and touched the object in the center and remained in this position for a few minutes, while the other objects continued to circle above. The object which had descended and touched the object in the center and which was lower, then rose and took its place with the other objects.

All of the objects then started to rise and what appeared to be newspapers came out of the object in the middle of the circling object. Then the sky seemed to rain lava, the lava coming from the object in the center and (X) headed the boat for shore. He stated that the lava coming from the object in the center appeared to be a white metal, and as it fell into the water, clouds of steam rose from the water. He stated that some of the lava landed on the beach. He also stated that his dog was killed and also a sea-gull in addition to his boy being hurt by the falling lava. (X) continued stating that (X) had said that he had taken pictures of the object and that if Mr (X) wanted them, he could have the negatives. (X) took Mr (X) to the home of his secretary that evening and showed him some of the disc fragments he had picked up, which were smooth on one side and rough on the other, according to Mr (X).

Mr (X) stated that he received a telephone call from the press upon returning to his hotel room, and that the press wanted to know about the flying disc fragments, and he told them that he was not talking until he had proved it. He stated he did not know how the press ever knew he was in Tacoma or had seen (X).

Mr (X) informed that at 9.30 am the next morning July 31, 1947 (X) and (X) appeared at his hotel room and again asked him to go home and forget about the discs, that his story was not false, but that he had had enough trouble. (X) said that his boy had been missed one morning and had been found at Lust, Montana, waiting on tables in a café; that he did not know how he had got there and that too

many things were happening. Mr (X) stated that
when (X) and (X) came to his hotel room, they had
an armful of fragments, and that (X) then informed
about how he had seen an object resembling those
seen by (X). (X) stated he had taken the patrol boat
on July 23, 1947, and had gone to Murray Island and
had found the beach littered with lava. (X) stated he
had looked up and had seen a balloon-like object
with portholes and windows, which had disappeared into a large cloud. Mr (X) stated that he
asked (X) again to see the pictures of the objects;
that (X) had again agreed to show them to him. Mr
(X) informed that he had then asked (X) if it would
be all right for him to call a friend, (X), who had also
seen some flying discs and let him see the fragments
and hear (X)'s story. (X) dissented, however, (X)
readily agreed. He also stated that he had placed a
call to Lieutenant Brown and Captain Davidson,
Army Intelligence officers at Hamilton Field, and
had asked them to come to his hotel, as they had
previously instructed him to report to them anything of an unusual nature or of interest regarding
the flying discs.

He stated that he flew to Seattle and that
Lieutenant Brown and Captain Davidson had come
to his room about 4.00 pm. (X) advised that he had
asked Lieutenant Brown just what he had found out
regarding the discs, and Lieutenant Brown had confidentially informed him that they had obtained a
picture of a disc, which appeared to be authentic,

which picture was taken by a man in Phoenix, Arizona. The picture, according to Lieutenant Brown, was of a circular object with a hole in the center, and of another object that looked like a flying wing. He stated that when Lieutenant Brown told him this, that he immediately thought of the object seen by Dahl. He stated that after hearing (X)'s story, Lieutenant Brown and Captain Davidson's attitude had changed immediately, and that they appeared disinterested. It was then suggested that they all go to Murray Island and look for the disc fragments. Lieutenant Brown and Captain Davidson stated that they had to return to Hamilton Field immediately. Mr (X) stated that Lieutenant Brown and Captain Davidson were very careful to gather up all of the fragments which had been brought to the room by (X).

He stated that the next morning he received a call from (X) who told him that Lieutenant Brown and Captain Davidson had been killed in a B-25 crash. He stated he did not know how (X) knew who had been in the plane before anyone else. He also stated that during the above conference numerous telephone calls were received from the press wanting to know about the conference. He stated that someone kept tipping the press off as to what was going on and what was being said daily verbatim. He informed that United Press men at Tacoma appeared to know all that took place during the conference, and even knew of the B-25 crash and those aboard, before the army released this information. Mr (X) informed that when he received news of the crash, that he and (X) fully expected to be contacted by Army Intelligence, as they were the last people with Lieutenant Brown and Captain Davidson. However, they were never contacted.

He further stated that he and (X) went down to the United Press to see what the survivors of the crash had informed about the crash and (X) told them that the B-25 had not crashed, but had been shot down, also that an Army informant had said that an observer at Kelso, Washington, had seen the plane throw out a landing flare after the two survivors had jumped from the plane, and that the plane had gone into a steep dive and dove into a hillside, and further that one engine had been on fire, but that the fire apparatus, protecting the engine, had failed to function. Mr (X) stated that (X) then came to see him and told him to go home and forget all about the discs, that such things as the B-25 crash had been happening to him all along.

Mr (X) stated that he then called the editor at Chicago and told him that the deal was off and that if he wanted his $200 back, he could have it; that two men had been killed and he was frightened of the whole thing. He stated that the editor informed him that it was all right with him to keep the $200. However, he would send him an additional check for the trouble he had been put to. Mr (X) advised that previous to this telephone call he had called his friend, (X) of the *Chicago Times,* and had told him that he did not have any faith in Army Intelligence and for him to conduct an investigation on (X) and get to the bottom of this disc fantasy. Mr (X) also advised that previous to the two above telephone calls, he had asked the press to investigate (X), as Army Intelligence had informed him that they could not find (X) and knew nothing concerning him, and appeared not to be interested in him, who seemed to know more about the flying discs than anyone else.

Mr (X) stated that he personally thinks that (X)'s business is a blind for something else and that (X) will do anything that (X) asks him to and will not talk unless (X) tells him to. Mr (X) stated that he still wanted to get to the bottom of the disc fragment story, so he and (X) had decided to go to Murray Island on Sunday August 3, 1947. However, when (X) was approached in this regard, and they had gone to the boat house where (X) kept his boat, (X) could not seem to make the boat run, and after making some excuses that he had to return to his office, had stated that he would return in about an hour, and by that time his mechanic should have the boat repaired and they could all proceed to Murray Island. Mr (X) informed that (X) never returned, and that they were unable to locate him at any of the telephone numbers he had given them.

They located (X) in a movie, according to Mr (X), and that (X), after making some efforts to locate (X), had informed them that (X) had left town for a few days. He further informed that about this time the grass contacted them and told them an informant had called and told them that (X) was on his way to Alaska in an Army plane.

Mr (X) advised that Captain (X) had informed him that he had made an appointment with Major (X) at McChord Field and intended to tell Major (X) the complete story. During the afternoon, Captain (X) and Major (X) came to the hotel room, according to Mr (X), and some of the fragments that (X) had brought to Mr (X)'s room, following the conference, were shown to Major (X). Upon viewing the fragments, Major (X), according to Mr (X), stated that they were nothing but slag from the copper mill. However, before Major (X) left, he gathered up every fragment in the room, according to Mr (X), and took them with him. Mr (X) stated that he then left for Boise, Idaho.

Mr (X) then produced a letter dated August 5, 1947, from (X) in which (X) attempts to encourage Mr (X) to continue his investigation into the flying discs. This letter is also being enclosed to the Bureau [see p. 93]. Mr (X) also gave SA (X) a copy of the article sent to him and to the Commanding Officer, Wright Field, Dayton, Ohio, regarding his sighting of the nine discs near Mount Rainier on June 24, 1947. Mr (X) advised that he is vitally interested in this matter and knows that there must be something to the flying discs story. He stated that he would do everything in his power to help the Bureau in this matter. Mr (X) stated that he has told the above story to Army Intelligence and Major (X) and to no one else, with the exception of (X).

Mr (X), Boise, Idaho advised that the (X) has never paid him for any news item that he has given them and he has never approached them in this manner. He stated that the (X) is not attempting to push the flying disc story, but merely attempting to get to the bottom of the flying discs story as they sincerely believe there is someone who knows the story of the discs and that they actually exist, and that the Army, when approached for information, merely state that they know nothing concerning them. Mr (X) also informed that Lieutenant Brown and Captain Davidson had contacted him on July 20, 1947 at Boise, Idaho regarding the discs and that is how he met them.

Unless advised to the contrary, no additional investigation is being conducted in this matter, and it is being considered as Referred upon Completion to the Seattle Office.

To Mr (X), Boise, Idaho

Dear Mr (X)   June 26, 1947
I have just read an account in the *Chicago Tribune* concerning an aerial train composed of at least nine units shaped like a pie-plate and silvery in color, traveling at 1,200 mph near Mount Rainier, as witnessed by you while flying in the vicinity.

This is quite important to me, because I have in my possession numerous independent confirmations of what you saw, although none in as great detail as your account. I am interested in publishing an article in our magazine, written from a personal account by yourself, and accompanied by pix of yourself, plane and rough sketches by yourself, of what you saw.

If you care to do this for me, I am prepared to pay our usual rates of 2 cents per word, plus $5.00 for each photograph you can provide, or for each sketch which can be used by our art staff to illustrate the article.

Included in this material, we'd like a short biographical sketch of yourself as "author background" material. The article would appear under your byline.

If you are not interested, I would at least appreciate a letter from you, confirming the newspaper story.

> (X), Editor
> *Venture Press*
> *Evanstown, Illinois*

To Mr (X), Boise, Idaho

Dear Mr (X),   August 5, 1947

It seems that (X) of the *Chicago Times* got the story from (X), because he called me, told me he was running it. I knew only what you'd told me over the phone. Now, it seems the newspapers are pestering the very devil out of all you fellows. (X) wired me for instructions, and I told him to say nothing to the newspapers, because he'll look silly if the Army explains this as meteors or something like that.

I don't blame you for being alarmed, but I trust you've had no trouble in your flying since then. Let's get that straight—there's no horrible plot involved. It's probably true that the two men killed were just accidents. It could be true that it was not an accident, but I don't think there was any connection with the disks, or anything of that nature, nor is the material from Murray Island to blame.

Certainly I don't think you'd suffer from completing your report on your mission, and sending me your affidavit. Also, you'll have some money coming for that, and no sense to tossing that out of the window. It is unfortunate that the thing seemed so big you had to call in Army Intelligence, but it will take them a long time to proceed to the point I've reached with this disk mystery. You see, you aren't the first to see them. They've been known for nearly 40 years, and I have ample proof of that. But your experience was the first real break towards a solution. I'd hate to have you drop the matter when all [that is] remaining to do is to file your report with me.

(X) is willing to contribute his share. I hope you will too. This thing *must not* be hushed up and forgotten. It's much too important to the people of America, if not the world. And no censorship of the matter is legal. You needn't fear that angle. You certainly did a bang-up job of investigation, also you wrote one of the best articles about your June 24 experience I've ever seen. Please do the same on this last business. You owe it to those two men who were killed.

I'd also like to know what developed on those pictures you took of those "discs", or whatever they were. In short, I'd like to have you continue to keep in contact with me, and relay to me anything further you learn. In turn, I'll give you the whole story, which I'm just about ready to break (not in the newspapers). And if it was as dangerous as you seem to suspect, I'm afraid I'd have been a corpse long ago.

But, and this is all you need remember, those disks are not red corpuscles in your eyeball, and they are not something you can forget about with an ostrich in the sand attitude. We've got to solve them, public hysteria or no. As for that hysteria, if laughing is hysteria, that's all the hysteria I've noticed.

You know your business, and you handled it like a major. But I'm hoping you do the easy part now and get that report on paper.

A check for your June 24 article is going out to you.

(X), Editor
Venture Press
Evanstown, Illinois

*Office memorandum of the US Government to Director
FBI. Attention: Assistant Director D. M. Ladd*

From: SAC, San Francisco   August 28, 1947

Subject: Reports of flying discs

On August 27, 1947, Lieutenant-Colonel (X), A-2,
Fourth Air Force, Hamilton Field, California,
advised that the Area Intelligence Requirements
Division Office of the Assistant Chief of Staff, A-2
Headquarters, requested that (X) of Phoenix,
Arizona, be completely interviewed in connection
with a report that he had seen on July 7, 1947, what
he believed were flying discs. (X) is supposed to
have taken several pictures of the discs with a 620
box camera.

A previous report of this reported sighting of
flying discs was forwarded the Bureau on August 8,
1947.

Colonel (X) has advised that (X), an intelligence agent of A-2 stationed at Long Beach,
California, would arrive in Phoenix, Arizona, on or
about September 2, 1947, and would be instructed
to contact the Phoenix Field Division Office.

In accordance with Bureau Bulletin No. 42,
Series 1947, it is felt that an agent from the
Phoenix Field Division should interview (X) of
Phoenix, if he has not already been interviewed.
Colonel (X) indicated that Mr (X) should, if possi-
ble, sit in on this interview.

SEPTEMBER, 1947

Office memorandum of the US Government to Director FBI

From: SAC, Butte   September 2, 1947
Subject: Flying discs, Remytel August 20, 1947
With reference to the above-described teletype, Mr (X) of Twin Falls, Idaho, was the principal source of information. Mr (X), who is the Executive Director of the (X), explained that he and his wife

and Mrs (X), a neighbor, were sitting on their front porch at approximately 9.30 pm, August 19,1947. He said that Mrs (X) suddenly shouted and pointed to the sky and thereafter stated that she had seen an object traveling at a terrific rate of speed in a northeasterly direction. The object was out of sight before Mr (X) and Mrs (X) could see anything.

While they were discussing what Mrs (X) had seen, approximately 10 minutes later, all three saw 10 similar objects proceeding rapidly in the same direction in the form of a triangle. As the group of objects was disappearing, three of the objects on the left flank peeled off and proceeded in a more northeasterly direction. The remaining objects appeared to close ranks and proceeded in a north-easterly direction.

From 3 to 5 minutes later these same individuals saw another group of three objects proceeding in the same direction, and again in the shape of a triangle. From 3 to 5 minutes later all three observed another group in a triangular formation consisting of five or six objects. They were proceeding in the same direction.

A few minutes later the three persons saw a large group of objects estimated at from 35 to 50 flying in a triangular formation in the same direction. Approximately 20 or 25 minutes after the large group of objects was observed, similar objects were noted coming back over the city in a south-westerly direction. These objects were generally in groups of three, five and seven and followed each other at approximately 5 minute intervals.

Mrs (X) called Detective (X) of the Twin Falls Police Department, a next-door neighbor, who was then accompanied by two others also members of the Twin Falls Police Department. The three officers watched for a few minutes and observed a group of about 12 objects flying in formation over the city in a southwesterly direction. The members of the Police Department did not continue watching, although Mr (X) later saw other groups, which were also seen by the (X)s and Mrs (X). Mrs (X) had also called her husband, who saw some of the objects.

On the night in question the sky was overcast and the objects could not be seen closely; however, they were distinct enough so that all persons could observe what they described as a glow going through the air. They said that the objects appeared to be lighted from the inside and were of a color similar to regular electric lights.

Detective (X) and Mr (X) both stated that they could not be meteors or comets, that they flew on a level line and did not appear to drop. They flew at a terrific rate of speed and were visible for only a few minutes at a time. Both persons interviewed said that the objects could not have been geese or ducks and that the lights were not a reflection of the city lights on some other object.

None of the persons interviewed noticed any flames or anything except the glow of lights. None of the persons who claimed to have seen these objects were drinking at the time. No other persons in Twin Falls reported seeing the objects mentioned herein; however, Mr (X) and Mr (X) stated that it was purely by accident that they had seen the objects and that they would not have seen them unless they were looking for them, because of the speed at which they traveled. On account of the overcast sky they were unable to estimate the size of the objects or the height at which they flew.

No further investigation is being conducted by the Butte Office, and the case is being closed.

Office memorandum of the US Government to Director, FBI

From: SAC, San Francisco   September 4, 1947
Subject: Reports of flying discs
Enclosed is a copy of a letter dated August 28, 1947, from Lt Col (X) of A-2, Hamilton Field, California, with an attachment referring to the sighting of a flying object by Captain (X) and his co-pilot, (X), near Bethel, Alaska.

Photostatic copies of this letter and attachment are being forwarded to the Anchorage Field Office. In accordance with Bureau Bulletin No. 42, dated July 30, 1947, Anchorage is requested to interview Captain (X) and his co-pilot, (X), preferably separately, in order to obtain all details of their reported sighting of a flying object on August 4, 1947. The San Francisco Field Office should be furnished two copies of the results of these interviews for distribution to the Sixth Army Intelligence.

To Commanding General, Fourth Air Force,
San Francisco, California

August 19, 1947

Subject: Matters of national interest

The attached letter has been received from the Alaska Communication System station at Bethel, Alaska. It is submitted for your information.

SVEND C. HANSEN
Captain, Signal Corps
Acting Executive, Alaska Communication
System, Signal Corps, Seattle, Washington

To Special Agent in Charge, FBI, San Francisco,
California

August 28, 1947

Forwarded for your information.

DONALD L. SPRINGER
Lt Colonel
HQ Fourth Air Force
Hamilton Field, California

*To Commanding Officer, Alaska Communication
System, Seattle 4, Washington*

August 5, 1947

Subject: Matters of national interest

The following report is submitted on a matter which may become of national interest. (X) and his co-pilot (X) have stated that on August 4, 1947 they sighted and followed a flying saucer northwest of Bethel, Alaska. This object was bigger than the Douglas DC-9 they were flying, and crossed their course at right angles to them. It was flying at an altitude of 1,000 feet. They swung in behind it and followed it at an air speed of 170 mph, but it was out of sight in 4 minutes. They state the object was smooth-surfaced and streamlined with no visible means of propulsion whatever.

It is realised that the Fourth Air Force claims there are no such things but (X) is not a man given to exaggeration. In view of the excellent reputation of (X) and the fact that no one here doubted in the least but that he actually saw this object, this report is turned in for any action deemed necessary by your office.

HAROLD D. JOHNSON
*Signal Corps
Operator in Charge*

Office memorandum of the US Government to Director FBI

From: SAC, Seattle   September 12, 1947

Subject: Flying disks reported by Bruce Armstrong and M. A. Nichols, Seattle, Washington, August 12, 1947: Security matter X

The newspaper, *Seattle Post Intelligencer*, carried an article in the morning issue of August 13 reporting the sighting of flying discs. The article appeared on the fifth page and was headed "Blue triangle latest thing seen in disks." Under this caption was a short write-up which stated, in substance, that one Bruce Armstrong, an electronics technician, and a number of other engineers at Boeing Aircraft had sighted a mysterious flying object about 2.30 pm on August 12. The newspaper report further stated that the object seemed to be fluttering like a leaf, and appeared to be a black or dark-blue triangular substance. In this article also appeared another report of a disk supposedly sighted by one M. A. Nichols, 1125 SW 102nd Street, Seattle, and Nichols described it as a big ball reflecting light, giving it a purplish tinge.

Interview with Bruce Armstrong on August 13 revealed that Armstrong was standing in front of Section D of the Boeing Aircraft plant with about 10 other research engineers and had noticed a small black object flying about 200 feet high, going south over Boeing Field runway. Armstrong further

stated, upon interview, that the object appeared triangular in shape and floated in the air like a leaf,
and he estimated the speed to be about 15 mph.
Armstrong could not accurately determine the distance between him and the object, but it is noted
that Section D is about half a mile from the oppo-
site side of Boeing Field where he supposedly had
sighted it.

The other research engineers were also interviewed regarding this object. The consensus of these
men was that the object resembled a black leaf in
flight and looked more like a piece of tarpaper than
anything. When the object reached the end of the
runway in Boeing Field it climbed into the sky in a
southwesterly direction and disappeared.

Mr (X), operator of the control tower for the
Northwest Airlines, was then contacted. He stated
that he reviews all reports of objects seen in the
vicinity of the field and makes a log of such. He
reviewed his log but could not see any record of
such an item, but upon contact with Mr (X) who
was on duty at the time the object was supposedly
sighted, the following information was obtained:
He stated that about 2 o'clock in the afternoon
there were several pieces of burnt paper which flew
over the field, and he did recall a large piece of
burnt paper which the wind had blown across the
runway and down the south end of the field. He
estimated that the paper was approximately 3 feet
in length. He stated that undoubtedly this was the

object in question, and inasmuch as the control tower has a complete view of the area in which the engineers had sighted this object, if anything further was noted it would have appeared in the log.

(X) was then interviewed regarding his report of a flying object. He stated that about 4 pm on August 12 he had sighted an object which he estimated to be about 35,000 feet in the air, which was flying over his home in a southwesterly direction. A neighbor, (X), also saw the object and examined the same with a pair of binoculars. According to (X), the object looked like a white dock moving, cylindrical in shape, and reflected the light of the sun with a sort of purplish tinge. Other witnesses who had seen the object at this time were (X) and (X) of Seattle, and their version of the object corresponded with that of (X).

Contact with (X) of the Seattle Weather Bureau Office at Boeing Field, revealed that weather balloons are released every six hours from his field commencing at 1.30 am. The balloons, according to Mr (X), are of a white gum color and reflect the light of the sun at a high altitude. Although Mr (X) could not understand why a balloon could have been sighted at 4 pm, he nevertheless was certain that, from the description of the object seen by these people, it must have been either one of his balloons or one released from some other area in the vicinity.

No further investigation is being conducted in this matter by this office.

Office memorandum to Director, FBI

From: SAC, Seattle   September 13, 1947
Subject: Flying disc sighted July 29, 1947 near Canyon Ferry, Montana by (X). Security matter X. Enclosed herewith for information of Bureau and Butte Division are copies of the following received September 2, 1947, from (X), Fourth Air Force, S-2, McChord Field, Washington: letter to Military Intelligence Division, USA, McChord Field, Washington from (X), dated August 8, 1947, with enclosure of report on a "flying saucer."

No action taken by Seattle.

To Military Intelligence Division, USA, McChord Field, Washington

Gentlemen,   August 8, 1947
Following the reading of an account of the visit of Mr Kenneth Arnold, Boise, Idaho, as published in the *Spokesman Review* under date of August 7, 1947, the undersigned considered the enclosed account of an observation of a "flying saucer" would be of interest to you.

This account has not been given to any newspaper or other publication as yet.

R. J. MADDEN
Division Plant Engineer
The Pac. Tel. & Tel. Co.
Spokane, Washington

Report on a "Flying saucer"
At or about 12.05 pm, July 29, 1947, a sedan, driven by Steve Hermann and carrying R. J. (Bob)
Madden in the front seat and Karl Hermann in the
rear seat, was proceeding northwesterly along the
road leading from Canyon ferry to York, both in
Montana some 25 miles northeast of Helena.

When at a point approximately ¼ mile NW of
Canyon Ferry (as shown on Forest Service Map to
be in the NE¼ of NE¼ of Sec. 10 T10N R1W),
Karl suddenly shouted "See it! See it! There's a flying saucer!" Steve immediately slowed down and
gradually brought the sedan to a stop, he and Bob
meanwhile scanning the sky in the direction
pointed by Karl in an effort to see the "flying
saucer", but without success.

Approximately 10 seconds elapsed between the
time Karl reported seeing the "saucer", coming
over the horizon at high speed from the southwest
(Karl first thought it a meteor) and traveling northeasterly, and the bringing of the car to a stop.

As the car came to a stop, Steve, Karl and Bob,
simultaneously, saw the following: Directly ahead,
(NW), 2 to 3 miles distant and approximately 3,000
feet above the ground, a bright disc hovering and
fluttering in the air. Descending and rising through
a vertical distance of 50 or a 100 feet for a period of
about 5 seconds then, while at the top of an ascent,
the disc suddenly swooped to the northeast at
tremendous speed and disappeared into the clear air

within a distance of 200 feet. That is to say, it did not pass beyond an obstruction to further visibility but "melted into thin air" as if because of tremendous speed. This disc was, from the viewpoint of the observers, apparently 3 feet in diameter, circular and of no great thickness — approximately 3 or 4″.

The sky was blue with scattered small clouds, the sun was shining brightly and the disc gleamed and shimmered in the bright sunlight as if covered with highly polished nickel.

After the "disc" disappeared from view, the sedan and its occupants proceeded northwesterly along the road, but could discern no evidence of the presence of the "disc" along or adjacent to that therefore.

It is to be remembered that the dimensions as stated above were as they appeared to the observers some 2 or 3 miles from the "disc" and the true dimensions must be considerably greater.

Office memorandum of the US Government to Director FBI

From: SAC, Salt Lake City   September 15, 1947
Subject: Flying discs, Remytel 10th instant
On September 10, 1947 an item relative to flying saucers appeared in the *Salt Lake Tribune* indicating that two young couples, Mr and Mrs Gaylon Caldwell and Mr and Mrs Richard Anderson, Logan, Utah, who had been playing bridge,

reported that they saw three brief flights of saucers, the first at 10.40 pm and two more before 11.10 pm, the evening of September 8, 1947. This news article also contained the names of Keith Hughes, Joan Crookston and Mr and Mrs Fred Thunell of Logan who had likewise made separate reports of having observed these flying discs.

Mr and Mrs Richard Anderson, when interviewed by an agent of this office, advised that they, in company with Mr and Mrs Gaylon Caldwell, observed approximately a dozen objects flying in group formation at about 2,000 or 3,000 feet in the air. They stated that they first observed these objects on September 8, 1947 at 10.30 pm when their bridge game broke up and both couples went out on the porch. The Andersons believed these objects to be similar in size to pigeons and stated that they seemed to be rather white and illuminated. They informed that the objects could have been birds; however, they appeared to be moving faster than birds as they circled the city in approximately 1–2 minutes, and then disappeared in a northern direction.

Mr and Mrs Anderson claimed to have observed no wing movement during the flight, and are unable to make up their minds as to exactly what they saw. Mr Anderson informed that Mr and Mrs Caldwell are presently en route to an unknown city in Nebraska.

Mr Keith Hughes and Joan Crookston both advised that they were unable to state how their names appeared in the newspaper as having observed flying saucers, inasmuch as neither had ever had the opportunity to view these flying objects, and the newspaper report was erroneous.

Mrs Fred Thunell advised that she, her husband, and five other couples had observed flying objects between 10.30 and 11.00 pm on the evening of September 8, 1947. She stated that they saw five groups, each containing 35 to 60 small objects, which were rather yellowish-white in color and were circling the city at a high rate of speed. Mrs Thunell stated that these objects were several thousand feet in the air and it was impossible for them to determine the size due to the distance, speed and cloud conditions.

Mrs Thunell informed that Mr and Mrs Norman Hall, Mr and Mrs H. P. Anderson, and Mrs Bessie Hendricks were present and observed the flying objects; however; none of them were able to determine what these objects might have been.

Mr and Mrs Norman Hall, Logan, Utah, advised that they viewed flying objects traveling clockwise above the city at approximately 10.30 pm the evening of September 8, 1947. They informed that they first believed the objects to be lights of an airplane. However, these objects seemed to change in formation and appeared to be similar to a group of moving stars. Mr and Mrs Hall believed that these objects were traveling much faster than birds.

It was determined that Mr and Mrs H. P. Anderson and Mrs Bessie Hendricks were not available for interview.

(X), Military Intelligence Division, Fort Douglas, Salt Lake City, Utah, is being advised by letter of the results of this investigation.

In view of the indefinite information furnished relative to this matter, no further investigation is being conducted by this office.

Office memorandum of the US Government to Director, FBI

From: SAC, San Francisco   September 15, 1947
Subject: Reports of flying discs
Reference is made to my letter dated August 26, 1947. Enclosed is a copy of a letter dated September 9, 1947 from Lt Colonel (X) of A-2, with a memorandum prepared by (X), Fourth Air Force CIC on August 20, 1947 and August 26, 1947. The memorandum contains information regarding observations of (X) of Sacramento, California.

Also enclosed is a letter dated September 10, 1947 from Colonel (X) with attachment dated September 9, 1947.

For the information of the Bureau, (X) of Boise, Idaho, who has been repeatedly interviewed in this matter by A-2, has expressed his intention to A-2 of selling for publication his detailed account of his investigation of flying discs.

To Special Agent in Charge, FBI, San Francisco,
California

September 9, 1947
Subject: Investigation of flying discs
Attached memorandum for your information.
DONALD L. SPRINGER
Headquarters Fourth Air Force
Office of the Assistant Chief of Staff
Intelligence (A-2)
Hamilton Field, California

Telephone message received from (X), *Oakland Tribune*, 1030 hours, August 18, 1947:
(X), Sacramento 2, California, and insurance executive with the firm of McGuire and Mills of Sacramento, reported the following incident:

At 4 pm on August 14, while driving on Cedar Ravine Road, 4 to 5 miles southeast of Placerville, California, he, accompanied by his wife, observed a "vapor" trail moving from north to south. Closer observation revealed a piece of "shiny metal" at from 600 to 1,000 feet altitude moving at a "high rate of speed". The object appeared to be more "rocket-shaped" than disc-shaped. It appeared to be approximately 5 feet in length and was "tilted in a semi-circle".

The object struck the ground with a "puff of black smoke" about 100 feet below the top of a hill which was approximately 750 feet ahead of

the automobile driven by the observer. An inter-
vening canyon prevented investigation of the
location where the object was observed to have
landed.

The observer is able to identify the location
where the object was observed to land. (X) is a
University of California graduate, and is personally
known by members of the *Oakland Tribune* staff. He
is a brother-in-law of (X) of southern California.

Memorandum for the officer in charge

1. On 20 August 1947, this agent and Special Agent
    Hubbard interviewed (X), at his home in
    Sacramento, California, and he stated in sub-
    stance that on the afternoon of August 14, 1947,
    he was driving his automobile from Placerville,
    California, on the Cedar Ravine Road. His wife
    was in the front seat of the automobile and (X)'s
    mother and the two Switzer children were in the
    back seat of the car. At about 1600 hours they
    were at a point approximately 5 miles south-west
    from Placerville when (X) saw a white smoke
    trail out of the corner of his eye. In searching for
    a rocket ship (P-80), he saw an object, 4 to 6 feet
    in length, 10″ to 14″ wide, and of a metal color,
    bright like highly polished chromium. In rela-
    tion to the travel of the automobile the object
    was first seen at 1030, and when the object
    reached a point at approximately 1200, it was

engulfed in a puff of dark-gray smoke about 10 feet in diameter. The object was traveling at a terrific rate of speed and seemed to be in a very shallow dive. When the puff of smoke appeared, the object disappeared completely and there were no particles seen to have fallen from the smoke. The point where the object was engulfed in the smoke was about 800 yards distant (in front of (X)) with no possibility of the object being hidden from view by vegetation or terrain. The object appeared rectangular in shape, except for one very short period of time it appeared to have a top surface that was very slightly curved. (X) turned to tell his wife about the object and found her with her mouth open in an effort to say something and with her hand in a pointing gesture toward where the object had disappeared. The object was not very high in relation to the terrain and seemed to be following the contour of a canyon.

2. In a separate interview (X) concurred in the information obtained from (X) with the following exceptions: The smoke trail and the puff that engulfed the object appeared dark-gray in color and there was no change in the color. (X) estimated the object to be about 5 feet long and about a foot wide, with the top surface being slightly curved. The object appeared to be somewhat larger in front than in the rear.

Agent's notes:

At the time this object was seen, the sun was to the back, the sky was clear and the object gave off a very bright reflection. (X) has been connected with the field of insurance investigation for the last 18 years and appears to be a man not desirous of publicity. The other passengers of the car did not see the object. (X) is in the process of moving to a ranch near Placerville, California, and his new address will be in Eldorado County, California. Arrangements have been made to meet (X) at 1400, 26 August, 1947 at Placerville, California, for the purpose of going back over Cedar Ravine Road to locate the point where the object disappeared. (X) will communicate with the AC of S, A-2, Headquarters Fourth Air Force, Hamilton Field, California, if any information regarding wreckage of an aircraft is located in the area in question. (X) was not informed of the mission and was led to believe that the mission was an effort to locate possible aircraft wreckage in the area.

DRYDEN MOON
Special Agent, AF CIC

3. On August 26, 1947, Special Agent Hubbard and this agent contacted (X) at Placerville, California. After traveling Cedar Ravine Road to a point 9 miles southeast of Placerville, known as Buck's Bar, (X) decided that the place from where he had observed the object on August 14,

1947 was nearer to Placerville. After a thorough check of the road, (X) believed the spot where he had observed the object to be on the ridge just north of Webber Creek where the road breaks over the summit. This point is 2 miles from the Raffels Hotel, Placerville, California, on the Cedar Ravine Road. As the road approaches the summit it curves to the left which would provide an observer from an automobile a sweeping view through 40° of the canyon and the horizon on the south side of Webber Creek. This point of observation lies 38° 42′ 45″ North Latitude and 120° 47′ 15″ West Longitude. The elevation at this point is 2,000 feet above sea level. The horizon from this point in the south is formed by a series of mountain peaks lying generally through 38° 39′ 45″ and which are on the south side of Squaw Hollow Creek, a distance of 4 miles, and ranging in elevation from 2,300 feet to 2,500 feet above sea level. (X) was not definite as to what part of the field of view he had seen the object and indicated that it could have been as far as the horizon. Any object, or particles of an object, that he saw, if on the ground on the field of view, would be in a 6-square-mile area of wooded, mountainous terrain which is full of canyons and ravines.

Agent's notes:
This agent believes that (X) could have seen an aluminium-surfaced conventional type aircraft which, due to the distances at which he observed it, distinguishing features were not seen because of the bright reflection and the short period of observation. The aircraft would have been coming from the left as (X) turned to the left, thereby giving the effect of a much greater speed than the object was really traveling. This agent has no explanation as to the smoke trail observed by (X). If reconnaissance is desired of the area to see if anything can be located on the ground, this agent suggests that a small-type aircraft, similar to an L-5, be used in low-level flight between the hours of 1100 to 1800. (X) was very cooperative and expended much of his own time in an effort to be of as much service as possible. (X) will communicate with the AC of S, A-2, Headquarters Fourth Air Force, Hamilton Field, California, in the event of any report of aircraft wreckage in the area.

4. On August 26, 1947, a check with the State Forest Service, Camino, California, and the Federal Forest Service, Placerville, California, provided the following information: there have been no forest fires or reported aircraft crashes in the area in question within the last month.

DRYDEN S. MOON
Special Agent, 4AF CIC

To Special Agent in Charge, FBI, San Francisco, California

September 10, 1947

Subject: Investigation of flying disc

Attached memorandum for your information.

DONALD L. SPRINGER
Lt Colonel, Air Corps
Deputy AC of S
Intelligence (A-2)
Hamilton Field, California

Memorandum for the officer in charge

(X), Berkeley, California, was interviewed September 8, 1947 at his place of employment, the University of California, concerning flying objects he reported to have seen on July 29, 1947 while with (X) of the 415th AAF. (X) stated in substance that he was a 1st Lt in the Reserve and that on July 29, 1947, shortly after 12 noon, he and (X) had just landed from a routine training flight when (X) called his attention to an unidentified flying object that was following a P-50 aircraft at a terrific rate of speed. (X) estimated the P-50 to be flying at approximately 250 mph on a preliminary approach to landing at Hamilton Field. In (X)'s estimation the object he saw following the P-50 maintained a speed of three to four times that of the aircraft. A moment later a second object appeared and flew a course described as something similar to a fighter aircraft's maneuvers when accompanying heavier ships, or a left to right movement, over the object first sighted. (X) stated that this maneuvering continued until the objects were out of sight. He estimated the time to be approximately 15 seconds, the course approximately 120 degrees. He could not estimate the size of the objects nor actual altitude, though he did not believe them to be beyond 6,000 feet. He described the objects as being milky-white in color, and unlike any conventional type aircraft he had ever seen. When questioned whether he was familiar with the Navy "Flapjack", (X) stated that he was, and that he was certain the objects he reported seeing were not of this nature.

Agent's notes:
(X) is a former officer of the US AAF and a B-29 pilot of considerable experience. He does not convey the impression of being the kind of person who would "imagine" that he was seeing objects, nor has he any apparent desire for publicity. (X) is in charge of (X) at Berkeley, California.

LESLIE S. HUBBARD
Special Agent CIC ADC
AAF

Office memorandum of the US Government to Director FBI

From: SAC, Anchorage   September 17, 1947

Subject: Flying disks

Reference is made to Bureau Bulletin No. 42 dated July 30, 1947. This is to advise that two army officers reported to the Office of the Director of Intelligence, headquarters Alaskan Department at Fort Richardson, Alaska, that they had witnessed an object passing through the air at a tremendous rate of speed which could not be judged as to mph.

The first officer stated that his attention was attracted to this airborne object, and he in turn pointed it out to the second officer. The object appeared to be shaped like a sphere and did not give the impression of being saucer-like or comparable to a disk. The first officer stated that it would be impossible to give minute details concerning the object, but that it appeared to be approximately 2 or 3 feet in diameter and did not leave any vapor trail in the sky.

Both officers attempted to determine the approximate altitude of the object, and from a weather group stationed nearby it was determined that cloud formations at the time the object was sighted were "scattered above 10,000 feet". The object was noted to be traveling below the cloud formation.

The first officer stated that in his opinion the object appeared to be metallic and was silver in color, much like the color of many airplanes.

The second officer stated substantially the same facts and also pointed out that the object remained within his vision for approximately 15 to 20 seconds. When sighted, the object was traveling due south at a speed considerably in excess of any plane. The second officer stated that the object appeared to him to be approximately 10 feet in diameter and compared it to half the size of a full moon on an ordinary night. The second officer based the altitude at approximately the same as the first officer except for the fact that due to the size he believed the object to be, he estimated the altitude to be only approximately 3,000 or 4,000 feet. The object appeared broadside to the second officer and no evidence of a spinning motion or reflection was noted. As to the color, the second officer pointed out that it appeared to be a dull metal finish.

In conclusion, the second officer pointed out that one of the remarkable features of this object was that it was definitely traveling against the wind.

The exact date of the sighting of this object was not furnished to this office, and inasmuch as it occurred previously to the receipt of Bureau instructions in this matter, no further investigation is being conducted by this office unless specifically requested to do so by the Bureau.

*Office memorandum of the US Government to
Director FBI*

From: SAC, Philadelphia   September 18, 1947
Subject: Flying object reported over Philadelphia
August 6, 1947. Sabotage; Remytel August 7 last.

(X) of Philadelphia, who is employed by the (X),
Philadelphia, advised as follows: Between 10.30 and
10.45 pm on August 6, 1947, she was sitting on the
steps of her home with (X). She was facing north
and observed a large white object traveling at a
very fast rate of speed to the south. There was a
buzzing sound, not too loud but plainly audible,
just after this object passed through the air. This
white object left in its trail a thin streak of smoke,
which was grayish in color.

Miss (X), Philadelphia, who is employed by the
(X) Inc., Philadelphia, stated she was sitting on the
steps of (X)'s home on the evening of August 6,
1947, around 10.45 pm engaging in conversation
with (X) when (X) abruptly stopped in the middle
of her conversation and appeared to be frightened.
(X) at that time was sitting in a position in which
she was facing south. She did not see any object in
the sky after noting (X)'s change of expression, but
she did hear a slight buzzing sound.

(X), Philadelphia, an insurance agent, who was a
former pilot of B-24s in the Army Air Corps, advised
as follows: He was sitting on the steps of his home
around 10.45 pm on August 6, 1947, with his wife;

and his neighbors, the (X) family, were sitting on their steps next door. All of the above parties were facing east. (X) notices at this time an object, emitting a bluish-white flame, passing quickly through the air. The object was traveling from northeast to south-west. Using his experience in the Army Air Corps as a guide, he estimated the above object was between 1,000 and 3,000 feet in the air and traveling at a rate of between 400 to 500 mph. This object did not lose elevation as it passed through the air and left either smoke or a condensation trail in its former path, which lasted for about 2 seconds. A hissing sound accompanied the passing of this object. This sound was moderate and not nearly as loud as the noise accompanying the passage of a rocket ship.

(X), who is a retired police officer of the Philadelphia Police Department, advised as follows: Around 10.45 pm on August 6, 1947, he and his wife were sitting on the steps of their home, when he noticed an object, resembling to him a giant firecracker, pass quickly through the air. He heard no noise, but the object had completely passed from view in a southern direction within a split second. It left a fiery trail for about 100 feet. August 6, 1947 was a clear night, and no storm was brewing. He was sure the object he saw was no falling star, and he noted the above object did not seem to be falling but maintaining the same altitude.

The wives of the two men verified the accounts of their husbands as to the above-mentioned object.

It is to be noted that the (X)s and the (X)s live in northeast Philadelphia near Oxford Circle, which is about 10 miles removed from the residence of (X). (X)'s residence is located in the western part of Philadelphia. The (X)s and (X)s are not known to the above-mentioned. It is further noted the observations of Miss (X), the (X)s and the (X)s roughly correspond. All of the above persons seem reliable and not the type to seek publicity or to spread rumors.

(X) called the *Inquirer*, Philadelphia newspaper, and inquired if it could offer an explanation as to what they had seen. A representative of that paper had advised the (X)s that the object they saw may have been some product of an oil refinery or chemical company in their neighborhood.

Both the offices of Naval Intelligence and Army Intelligence in Philadelphia were requested by the Philadelphia Office to ascertain if either the Army or Navy was doing any experimental work on new types of planes or equipment, in the vicinity of Philadelphia. Such was done with negative results.

All logical investigation having been conducted, no further action will be taken on the instant matter unless advised to the contrary by the Bureau.

To Director FBI, Washington DC. Attention: Assistant Director D. M. Ladd

Dear Sir,   September 19, 1947

I am transmitting herewith copies of a "restricted" letter dated September 3, 1947, which was furnished to me by Lieutenant Colonel (X), A-2, Army Air Forces, Hamilton Field, California, which letter is designated to certain Commanding Generals in the Army Air Forces from Colonel (X), Assistant Chief of Staff, Intelligence, Headquarters Air Defense Command, Mitchell Field, New York, concerning "Cooperation of FBI with AAF on Investigations of 'Flying Disc' incidents".

It is my understanding from recent Bureau instructions that we are to assist the Air Force Intelligence personnel in the investigations of flying disc incidents. However, it will be noted from the attached letter that it is Army interpretation that it was their intent that the Bureau would investigate those incidents of the so-called "discs" being found on the ground and apparently not those which are observed in flight. Further, the attention of the Bureau is respectfully called to paragraph two of this letter and to the last sentence therein which states, "The services of the FBI were enlisted in order to relieve the numbered Air Forces of the task of tracking down all the many instances which turned out to be ash can covers, toilet seats and whatnot."

In the first place, the instructions issued by the Army Air Forces in this letter appear to limit the type of investigations which the Bureau will be asked to handle, and secondly it appears to me the wording of the last sentence in the second paragraph mentioned above is cloaked in entirely uncalled-for language, tending to indicate the Bureau will be asked to conduct investigations only in those cases which are not important and which are almost, in fact, ridiculous.

The thought has occurred to me the Bureau might desire to discuss this matter further with the Army Air Forces both as to the types of investigation which we will conduct and also to object to the scurrilous wordage which, to say the least, is insulting to the Bureau in the last sentence of paragraph two.

In the event the Bureau decides to discuss the matter further with the Army Air Forces, it is recommended that no indication whatsoever be given indicating this letter was referred to me by Lieutenant Colonel (X), inasmuch as it would undoubtedly cause him serious embarrassment and would certainly cause the excellent personal relationship which exists between Lieutenant Colonel (X) and this office to be endangered.

HARRY M. KIMBALL
Special Agent in Charge
FBI San Francisco

To Commanding Generals, First, Second, Fourth,
Tenth, Eleventh and Fourteenth Air Forces.
Attention: Assistant Chief of Staff, A-2

September 3, 1947

Subject: Cooperation of FBI with AAF on investigations of "Flying Disc" incidents.

1. The FBI has agreed to assist Air Force Intelligence personnel in the investigation of "flying
   disc" incidents in order to quickly and effec-
   tively rule out what are pranks and to concen-
   trate on what appears to be a genuine incident.
2. It was the original intent of the AC/AS-2,
   Headquarters, Army Air Forces that whereas the
   ADC Air Forces would interview responsible
   observers whose names would be furnished by
   AAF, the FBI would investigate incidents of so-
   called "discs" being found on the ground. The
   services of the FBI were enlisted in order to
   relieve the numbered Air Forces of the task of
   tracking down all the many instances which
   turned out to be ash can covers, toilet seats and
   whatnot.
3. It is requested that each A-2 informally coordi-
   nate and cooperate with the FBI, generally
   keeping the FBI informed of any proposed calls
   that intelligence personnel will make on this
   subject. Very shortly, with the separation of the
   AAF from the War Department, a firm policy

will be established to clarify the liaison arrangement between A-2s and FBI Special Agents. Presently, it is considered inadvisable to promulgate a formal interim policy — only to have it replaced in a month or so by another.

By command of
LIEUTENANT GENERAL STRATEMEYER

To FBI, Washington DC

Gentlemen,   September 19, 1947

Lake Forest, Illinois: alleged violation of Section 2350, PL&R, by des Arc Foundation; sale of information on flying discs.

The subject involved in case of above description is (X), formerly of Lake Forest, Illinois, who may also have given a Chicago address at various times.

Can you advise whether you have a record of this man and if so, will you please forward a copy of it to me.

T. H. BARKOW
Post Office Inspector
Chicago 7
Illinois

To Inspector, Post Office Dept, Chicago 7, Illinois

September 24, 1947

Alleged violation of Section 2350, PL&R, by des Arc Foundation; sale of information on flying discs: Reference is made to your letter dated September 19, 1947, requesting information regarding one (X).

You are advised that an effective search cannot be conducted through the files of the Identification Division of the Federal Bureau of Investigation on the basis of name only. If you are able to furnish the physical description of (X) or other means of identification such as a registry number, a detailed search will be conducted in an effort to furnish you with the information desired.

FBI
Washington DC

Office memorandum of the US Government to Director FBI

From: SAC, Chicago   September 20, 1947

Subject: Flying discs (X) — informant

Reference is made to your letter dated August 11, 1947 in the above-captioned matter. (X), McHenry County, Woodstock, Illinois, advised that he had received no reports of flying discs in the community of Lily Lake, Illinois. He further stated that he had no record or knowledge of (X) of Lily Lake.

(X), Lily Lake, Illinois, advised that he was personally acquainted with (X), whom he described as a successful writer of mystery stories. He said he had no information to the effect that Shaver was mentally unsound and he believed him to be a substantial citizen.

(X) advised she had sold property to (X) on two occasions and was well acquainted with (X) and his wife. She knew of no derogatory information concerning him.

(X) was interviewed at Lily Lake, Illinois and advised that he was the feature writer of mystery stories for (X) magazine, which magazine is edited by (X), Chicago, Illinois. (X) at the outset stated that Palmer had told him the FBI would contact him regarding flying discs.

(X) indicated that the telegram received by the War Department, referred to in referenced letter, was probably sent by one of his readers, unknown to him. He said that he wrote mystery stories based on his firm conviction that under the earth are various caverns formerly inhabited by a super race, who have since fled to other planets. This region of caverns he calls Lemuria. He stated he believes there is valuable machinery and other resources in these caverns. He therefore explained flying discs, which he calls "space ships", as the mode of travel of the Lemurians coming from other planets to reclaim the valuable machinery. (X) indicated that his theories had aroused a wide following among readers of (X) magazine.

(X) exhibited an article from an edition of the *Chicago Times* for Sunday August 3, 1947. The article stated that on June 24, 1947, on Murray Island, off the Washington coast, there had occurred a mysterious explosion which was believed to have been caused by a guided missile or rocket. It further stated that the date of the explosion was that same date on which on Kenneth Arnold, a private pilot, sighted the first flying disc at Boise, Idaho.

The article went on to state that it was believed at the time that there was some correlation between the flying disc and the Murray Island explosion, and that Raymond Palmer, Chicago magazine editor, had employed Arnold to investigate and "cover" the Murray Island explosion.

The article went on to state that on August 1, 1947, at Tacoma, Washington, there was a conference among officials of the Army and Navy, who discussed the possible relation between the Murray Island explosion and the appearance of flying discs. Arnold was supposed to have been in attendance at this conference. At the conference, authorities brought a sample of a lava oxide metal, allegedly taken from the scene of the Murray Island explosion.

The article stated that following the conference, two pilots left by plane for Hamilton Field, California, carrying samples of the lava oxide metal. The article further reported that the plane crashed near Hamilton Field, California, and it was conjectured that the plane had exploded by reason of the combustion of the lava oxide metal it carried.

From the above newspaper article, it should be noted that (X)'s employer was from the start "exploiting" the appearance of the flying discs, possibly to enhance the appeal of (X)'s stories. It is possible therefore that the entire flying disc theory was conceived by (X).

Office memorandum of the US Government to
Mr Ladd

From: E. G. Fitch   September 23, 1947
Subject: Instrument found on farm near Danforth, Illinois.

Reference is made to a memorandum to Mr Harbo from Mr Baughman on the above-captioned matter, dated September 3, 1947. The reference memorandum indicates that the instrument has been examined by the laboratory and the laboratory had contacted a Mrs Whedon of the Army Engineers and she indicated that the instrument had been used by the Air Forces on tests which were classified as "Top Secret".

The memorandum indicates that Special Agent S. W. Reynolds of the Liaison Section contacted the Intelligence Division of the Air Forces and was advised that Mrs Whedon alluded that the instrument was used in "Operation Mogul". The instrument was loaned to the Intelligence Division of the Air Forces who in turn forwarded it to Wright Field. The report was received from Wright Field indicating the instrument had no connection with "Operation Mogul" or any other operation at Wright Field. It was classified as a hoax in view of this apparent discrepancy between information developed from Mrs Whedon and information received from Intelligence Division of the Air Forces that the Bureau might wish to pursue this further.

Mr Zimmers of the Technical Laboratory advised Mr Reynolds of the Liaison Section that Mrs Whedon had told him that a Major Hopkins handled the liaison in Washington for the tests in which this instrument was used. Lieutenant Colonel George Garrett of the Intelligence Division of the Air Forces advised Special Agent Reynolds that he contacted Major Hopkins. He advised that Major Hopkins has had a great deal of experience in radio and along technical lines. Major Hopkins advised Colonel Garrett that the instrument could not have been used in the "Operation Mogul". Hopkins indicated that from the pictures and particles recovered, it appeared to him to be a part or portions of an old-type radio loudspeaker.

In view of the information received from Major Hopkins, Colonel Garrett stated that he was at a loss to explain the actions of Mrs Whedon other than to say that she perhaps gave a false impression as to her knowledge of the instrument and the "Operation

Mogul". Garrett pointed out that in view of the report received from Wright Field, together with the statement made by Major Hopkins, he felt that there was sufficient evidence that this instrument was not used in any War Department classified project and that in all probability it was just a hoax.

Recommendation:
It is recommended that this memorandum be forwarded to the Technical Laboratory for their information.

Office memorandum of the US Government to Director FBI

From: D. M. Ladd   September 25, 1947
Subject: Flying discs
The Bureau was requested by the Air Force Intelligence to assist the Air Forces in attempting to arrive at an explanation of the above phenomena. The Air Force indicated that the alleged sightings of flying discs might have been made by individuals of Communist sympathies for the purpose of causing mass hysteria in the United States over the fear of a secret Russian weapon. The Bureau agreed to assist in the investigation of the reported sightings, and the Field was advised in Bureau Bulletin No. 42, Series 1947, dated July 30, 1947, that they should investigate each instance which was brought

to their attention of the sighting of a flying disc in order to ascertain whether or not it was a *bona fide* sighting, an imaginary one, or a prank. The results of the investigation conducted by the Bureau Field Offices in this matter have failed to reveal any indication of subversive individuals being involved in any of the reported sightings.

The Bureau has received a communication in the captioned matter from the Special Agent in Charge at San Francisco, dated September 19, 1947, which attached a "restricted" letter that was furnished confidentially to the SAC at San Francisco by Lieutenant Colonel Donald L. Springer, A-2, Army Air Forces, Hamilton Field, California, a copy of which is attached hereto [see p. 127]. It is noted that the letter, which is dated September 3, 1947, is signed "By Command of Lieutenant General Stratemeyer" by Colonel R. H. Smith, Assistant Chief of Staff Intelligence, Headquarters, Air Defense Command, Mitchell Field, New York, and is addressed to the Commanding Generals of the various Air Forces. This letter is entitled "Cooperation of FBI with AAF on Investigations of 'Flying Disc' Incidents".

This letter states that in substance that it was the original intent of the AC/AS-2, Headquarters, Army Air Forces that whereas the ADC Air Forces would interview responsible observers, the FBI would investigate incidents of so-called discs being found on the ground. Further, it indicates that the services of the FBI were enlisted in order to relieve the numbered Air Forces of the task of tracking down all the many instances which turned out to be "ash can covers, toilet seats and whatnot".

Recommendation:
It is recommended that the Bureau protest vigorously to the Assistant Chief of Air Staff 2. It is also recommended that the Bureau discontinues all activity in this field and that the Bureau Field Offices be advised to discontinue all investigations and to refer all complaints received to the Air Forces. A proposed Bulletin is attached for your approval [not included].

Office memorandum of the US Government to Director FBI

From: SAC, Butte   September 27, 1947
Subject: Flying discs sighted May 5, 1947 between Ellensburg and Seattle, Washington.
(X) of Montana State Prison, Deer Lodge, Montana, has advised the writer that while driving between Ellensburg and Seattle, Washington, about 3.30 pm on May 5, 1947, he sighted a silver object streaking across the sky. This was also seen by (X), convict chauffeur and another passenger. This object went into a nosedive and they thought it would crash. However, before reaching the earth it disintegrated,

leaving a long pillar of "gas" hanging in the sky. It was particularly odd because this remained in form and did not blow away. These three people observed it while they drove from 20 to 30 miles.

This smoky, gaseous pillar was a long way off and remained high in the air. (X) said that this silver object was traveling at an excessively high rate of speed and when it disintegrated it was still a long way from the earth. He said when he first saw it he thought it was probably a jet-propelled plane but that he couldn't tell except that its motions were erratic. He said he had not reported it until he noticed so much in the papers about these discs. Although three people saw it, they decided they must be "seeing things."

The Seattle Office is requested to advise Mr (X), Fourth Air Force, S-2, McChord Field, Washington. No further action is being taken by the Butte Office due to the time elapsing between the sighting of this object and the report.

To Major General George C. McDonald, Assistant Chief AS-2, The Pentagon, Washington DC

September 27, 1947

Dear General McDonald

The Federal Bureau of Investigation has been requested by your office to assist in the investigation of reported sightings of flying discs.

My attention has been called to instructions disseminated by the Air Forces relative to this matter. I have been advised that these instructions indicate that the Air Forces would interview responsible observers while the FBI would investigate incidents of discs found on the ground, thereby relieving the Air Forces of running down incidents which in many cases turned out to be "ash can covers, toilet seats and whatnot".

In view of the apparent understanding by the Air Forces of the position of the Federal Bureau of Investigation in this matter, I cannot permit the personnel and time of this organisation to be dissipated in this manner.

I am advising the Field Divisions of the Federal Bureau of Investigation to discontinue all investigative activity regarding the reported sightings of flying discs, and am instructing them to refer all complaints received to the appropriate Air Force representative in their area.

JOHN EDGAR HOOVER
Director FBI

OCTOBER, 1947

Internal memorandum

October 6, 1947

Flying discs

Effective immediately, the Bureau has discontinued its investigative activities as outlined in Section B of Bureau Bulletin No. 42, Series 1947, dated July 30, 1947.

All future reports connected with flying discs should be referred to the Air Forces and Bureau Agents should take no investigative action.

New titles in the series

The Compendiums

Each book in this handsome series consists of three key historical accounts, and is illustrated with maps and photographs.

The World War I Collection

The official inquiry into the disastrous military campaign at Gallipoli, plus the despatches of British generals at the front during the first nine months of the war, are presented here.
The Dardanelles Commission, 1914–16
Examines why, when British troops were already heavily deployed in France, the leaders of the day saw fit to launch a major offensive in the eastern Mediterranean.
British Battles of World War I, 1914–15
A collection of despatches written by British commanders in the field, mainly in northern France.

ISBN 0 11 702466 X   Price UK £14.99 US $19.95

The World War II Collection

Consists of three accounts of major milestones of World War II, written by the statesmen and military leaders of the day.
War 1939: Dealing with Adolf Hitler
Describes the policies of both Hitler and the British government in the months leading up to the outbreak of war.
D Day to VE Day: General Eisenhower's Report
General Eisenhower's personal account of the invasion of Europe, from June 1944 to May 1945.
The Judgment of Nuremberg, 1946
Focuses on the first trial of 21 major war criminals. The text describes the history, purpose and method of the Nazi party.

ISBN 0 11 702463 5   Price UK £14.99 US $19.95

The Siege Collection

The stories of four sieges involving British troops in the days of British Empire are presented here.

The Siege of Kars, 1855
This little-known siege lasted five months and took place during the Crimean War, in the mountains of eastern Turkey.

The Boer War: Ladysmith and Mafeking, 1900
Contains despatches describing the siege and relief of both Ladysmith and Mafeking, as reported by the commanders in the field. The reverses suffered at Spion Kop are included.

The Siege of the Peking Embassy, 1900
Tells the story of how the diplomatic staff in Peking, China, were besieged by the Boxers in 1900, and how they were rescued by an international force.

ISBN 0 11 702464 3   Price UK £14.99 US $19.95

Tragic Journeys

Features three of the most tragic journeys of the 20th century.

The Loss of the Titanic, 1912
The official inquiry presented here is the same report that was published in 1912. Also included is a reappraisal of the evidence relating to the SS *Californian*, the ship that failed to come to the rescue of the *Titanic*.

R. 101: The Airship Disaster, 1930
In its heyday, the airship R.101 was considered as glamorous as the *Titanic*. Sadly, its fate was equally tragic, as she crashed on her maiden flight to India. The official inquiry investigates why it all went so disastrously wrong.

The Munich Air Crash, 1958
Eight key players from the Manchester United football team died in this tragic accident at Munich airport in 1958. Included here are the official inquiries into the causes.

ISBN 0 11 702465 1   Price UK £14.99 US $19.95

The War Facsimiles

The War Facsimiles are exact reproductions of illustrated books that were published during the war years. They were produced by the British government to inform people about the progress of the war and the home-defence operations.

The Battle of Britain, August–October 1940

On 8 August 1940, the Germans launched the first of a series of mass air attacks on Britain in broad daylight. For almost three months, British and German aircraft were locked in fierce and prolonged combat in what has become known as the Battle of Britain. In 1941 the government published *The Battle of Britain* to explain the strategy and tactics behind the fighting that had taken place high in the sky over London and south-east England. Such was the public interest in this document, with its graphic maps and photographs, that sales had reached two million by the end of the war.

ISBN 0 11 702536 4   Price £4.99   US $8.95

The Battle of Egypt, 1942

Often referred to as the Battle of El Alamein, this battle was one of the major turning points for the Allies in World War II. The British, commanded by General Montgomery, were defending Egypt while the Germans under Rommel were attacking. This was a campaign the British could not afford to lose, because not only would it leave Egypt wide open for invasion, but it would also mean the loss of the Suez Canal and the oil fields. First published in 1943, *The Battle of Egypt* is an astonishing contemporary report of one of the most famous military victories in British history.

ISBN 0 11 702542 9   Price £5.99   US $10.95

Bomber Command: the Air Ministry account of Bomber Command's offensive against the Axis, September 1939–July 1941

Churchill declared on 22 June 1941: "We shall bomb Germany by day as well as by night in ever-increasing measure." Bomber Command of the RAF was to translate those words into action, beginning its attacks on Germany in May 1940, and steadily increasing its efforts as the war progressed. Published in 1941 at the height of World War II, *Bomber Command* tells the story of this fighting force during those early years.

ISBN 0 11 702540 2   Price £5.99   US $11.95

East of Malta, West of Suez: the Admiralty account of the naval war in the eastern Mediterranean, September 1939 to March 1941

This is the story of the British Navy in action in the eastern Mediterranean from September 1939 to March 1941 and their bid to seize control. During this time British supremacy was vigorously asserted at Taranto and Matapan. This facsimile edition contains contemporary maps, air reconnaissance photographs of the fleets and photographs of them in action.

ISBN 0 11 702538 0   Price £4.99   US $8.95

Fleet Air Arm: the Admiralty account of naval air operations, 1943

The Fleet Air Arm was established in 1939 as the Royal Navy's own flying branch. With its vast aircraft carriers bearing squadrons of fighter pilots, its main role was to protect a fleet or convoy from attack, or to escort an air striking force into battle. In *Fleet Air Arm*, published in 1943, the public could read for the first time of the expeditions of these great ships as they pursued and sank enemy warships such as the *Bismarck*.

ISBN 0 11 702539 9   Price £5.99   US $11.95

Land at War: the official story of British farming 1939–1944

Land at War was published by the Ministry of Information in 1945 as a tribute to those who had contributed to the war effort at home. It explains how 300,000 farms, pinpointed by an extensive farm survey, had been expected to increase their production dramatically, putting an extra 6.5 million acres of grassland under the plough. This is a book not just about rural life, but of the determination of a people to survive the rigours of war.

ISBN 0 11 702537 2   Price £5.99   US $11.95

Ocean Front: the story of the war in the Pacific, 1941–44

Ocean Front tells the story of the Allies' war against Japan in the central and western Pacific. Starting with Pearl Harbor in December 1941, this fascinating book recounts the Allies' counter-offensive, from the battles of the Coral Sea and Midway, to the recapture of the Aleutian Islands and the final invasion of the Philippines. Illustrated throughout with amazing photographs of land and sea warfare, *Ocean Front* provides a unique record of the American, Australian and New Zealand fighting forces in action.

ISBN 0 11 702543 7   Price £5.99   US $11.95

Roof over Britain: the official story of Britain's anti-aircraft defences, 1939–1942

Largely untold, *Roof over Britain* is the story of Britain's ground defences against the attacks of the German air force during the Battle of Britain in the autumn of 1940. First published in 1943, it describes how the static defences – the AA guns, searchlights and balloons – were organised, manned and supplied in order to support the work of the RAF.

ISBN 0 11 702541 0   Price £5.99   US $11.95

Other titles in the series

Rillington Place

" 'I want to give myself up. I have disposed of my wife.' 'What do you mean?' said the constable. Evans replied 'I put her down the drain.' The officer told Evans to think again before he said any more, and Evans said 'I know what I am saying. I cannot sleep and I want to get it off my chest.' "

Backdrop

The serial killer, or mass murderer, is often seen as a creation of modern society, but quiet killers, drawing no attention to themselves in the teeming streets of the metropolis, have been responsible for some of the most notorious crimes of the 20th century.

The Book

On 9th March 1950, Timothy Evans, of 10 Rillington Place, London, was hanged for the murder of his daughter Geraldine. His wife Beryl had also been murdered at the same time. Three years later, Reginald Christie, also of the same address, was hanged for the murder of his wife, Ethel. In the course of the investigation, five more bodies were discovered at 10 Rillington Place. Since then, doubts have been raised over the conviction of Timothy Evans. This government inquiry by Lord Brabin is an attempt to uncover the truth surrounding those macabre events that took place in 1949.

ISBN 0 11 702417 1   Price UK £6.99   US $12.95

Escape from Germany, 1939–45

*"It is quite certain that, apart from the microphone, no evidence what-
ever had been found to show a tunnel was being dug, yet in the
four-and-a-half months from the commencement of the tunnel
campaign, more than 166 tons of sand had been excavated from three
tunnels and hidden in a compound only a mile in circumference which
was constantly patrolled and inspected by Germans."*

Backdrop

The history of Air Force captivity in Germany began on 3
September 1939, the day Britain declared war on Germany. On
the same day, a New Zealand officer was shot down over the
North Sea and was subsequently taken prisoner. By December
1939, the numbers of those captured had grown, and the
Germans began to segregate Air Force prisoners, housing them in
special camps.

The Book

Of the 10,000 British airmen held as prisoners-of-war by the
Germans during World War II, less than 30 successfully managed
to find their way back to Britain or to a neutral country. After
1945, many escapers and PoWs were interviewed, and a file was
built up of their various experiences. This file was kept secret for
nearly 40 years (despite the fact that several famous films were
made about these escapes), as it was thought to contain evidence
of enterprise and resilience that could still be useful to an enemy.
Now "uncovered" for the public to read, this book contains the
true and often incredible stories of the heroic attempts of these
men to escape.

ISBN 0 11 702459 7   Price UK £6.99   US $14.95

Bloody Sunday, 1972: Lord Widgery's Report

"No order and no training can ensure that a soldier will always act wisely, as well as bravely and with initiative. The individual solider ought not to have to bear the burden of deciding whether to open fire in confusion such as prevailed on 30 January. In the conditions prevailing in Northern Ireland, however, this is often inescapable."

Backdrop

Northern Ireland forms part of the United Kingdom, and the Protestant majority of its population generally supports political union with Great Britain. However, many of the Roman Catholic minority would prefer union with the Republic of Ireland. This division has sparked much of the conflict between the two communities. In 1969, a British Army peace-keeping force was established in Northern Ireland.

The Book

On Sunday 30 January 1972, a protest march organised by the Northern Ireland Civil Rights Association took place in Londonderry, Northern Ireland, in the area of the Bogside and Creggan Estate. During the afternoon of that march, 13 civilians were killed by British soldiers, and another 13 were injured. As a result, a tribunal was appointed to inquire into the events which led up to this tragic loss of life. Heading the inquiry was Lord Widgery. This uncovered edition is the text of his report.

ISBN 0 11 702405 8   Price UK £6.99   US $10.95

The Irish Uprising, 1914–21: Papers from the British Parliamentary Archive

"Captain Bowen-Colthurst adopted the extraordinary, and indeed almost meaningless, course of taking Mr Sheehy Skeffington with him as a 'hostage'. He had no right to take Mr Sheehy Skeffington out of the custody of the guard for this or any other purpose, and he asked no one's leave to do so."

Backdrop
In 1914 it was still the case that the whole of Ireland was part of Great Britain, under the dominion of the King, and Irish constituencies were represented in the British Parliament.

The Book
This book contains five remarkable documents published by the British Government between 1914 and 1921, relating to the events leading up to the partition of Ireland in 1921. In the first, a report is made into the shooting of civilians following a landing of arms at Howth outside Dublin. The second is of the papers discovered relating to the activities of Sinn Fein and particularly of Sir Roger Casement. The third is the government inquiry into the Easter Rising of 1916. The fourth describes the treatment of three journalists by the British Army shortly after the uprising, and the last is an exchange of correspondence between Eamon de Valera and David Lloyd George prior to the Anglo-Irish Treaty of 1921.

ISBN 0 11 702415 5   Price UK £6.99   US $12.95

War in the Falklands, 1982

"On 22 March 1982 [10 days before the invasion], the Ministry of Foreign Affairs expressed concern at news of an insult to the Argentine flag at the LADE (Argentine Air Force airline) office in Port Stanley. The Governor reported that on the night of 20/21 March the LADE office had been entered, apparently by someone using a key. A Union flag had been placed over the Argentine flag there and 'Tit for tat, you buggers' written in toothpaste on a desk. In a later incident, during the night of 22/23 March, 'UK OK' was written on two external windows of the LADE office."

Backdrop

Since 1832, Britain has claimed sovereignty over the Falkland Islands in the South Atlantic. On 2 April 1982 Argentina invaded the Falklands and took possession of Port Stanley.

The Book

How did Britain come to have sovereignty over a small group of islands over 8,000 miles away? What were the events leading up to the Argentine invasion, and why was Britain caught so unprepared? What were the logistical problems involved in mounting a campaign to retake these islands? And how were feelings expressed about this extraordinary event?

These are just some of the issues which are dealt with by the archive material in this uncovered edition. Starting with the official government history of the Falkland Islands (from 1592, when the islands were first sighted), the book then gives the full text of Lord Franks' report, who was appointed in 1982 to investigate the events leading up to the invasion, and to review the way in which the Government discharged its responsibilities. A full description of the operation is included, and also the text of some famous debates in the House of Commons during this turbulent period.

ISBN 0 11 702458 9   Price UK £6.99   US $14.95

King Guezo of Dahomey, 1850–51

*"Retiring to our seats, the King insisted on our viewing the place of sacri-
fice. Immediately under the royal canopy were six or eight executioners,
armed with large knives, grinning horribly; the mob now armed with clubs
and branches, yelled furiously, calling upon the King to 'feed them – they
were hungry' . . . When it was all over, at 3 pm, we were permitted to
retire. At the foot of the ladder in the boats and baskets lay the bleeding
heads. It is my duty to describe; I leave exposition to the reader."*

Backdrop
In 1807, the British Parliament outlawed the trade in slaves,
followed in 1833 by an Act to abolish the institution of slavery.
However, in 1850, the slave trade was alive and well on the
west coast of Africa.

The Book
The fact that Africans were still being sold into slavery in the
mid-19th century was partly due to the reluctance of both the
merchants and the African chiefs to desist. King Guezo was one
of these African chiefs who profited by selling captives taken
during tribal wars. Although he was very friendly towards the
British, counting Queen Victoria as one of his most revered
friends, he was reluctant to give up his war-like habits. With
18,000 royal wives, an army composed in part of 3,000
Amazon women, and a warrior-like reputation to maintain, he
could see little attraction in farming as an alternative lifestyle.

Lord Palmerston was the Foreign Secretary who charged the
British Consul in west Africa with the unenviable task of per-
suading the African chiefs to give up their lucrative trade. Just
how the British managed to coerce the chiefs into abandoning
this practice is revealed in fresh and fascinating detail by these
contemporary despatches. They provide an astonishing glimpse
of the customs and way of life in Africa some 150 years ago.

ISBN 0 11 702460 0   Price UK £6.99   US $12.95

Uncovered editions: how to order

FOR CUSTOMERS IN THE UK
Ordering is easy. Simply follow one of these five ways:

Online
Visit www.clicktso.com

By telephone
Please call 0870 600 5522, with book details to hand.

By fax
Fax details of the books you wish to order (title, ISBN,
quantity and price) to: 0870 600 5533.
Please include details of your credit/debit card plus
expiry date, your name and address and telephone
number, and expect a handling charge of £3.00.

By post
Post the details listed above (under 'By fax') to:
The Stationery Office
PO Box 29
Norwich NR3 1GN
You can send a cheque if you prefer by this method
(made payable to The Stationery Office). Please include
a handling charge of £3 on the final amount.

TSO bookshops
Visit your local TSO bookshop (or any good bookshop).

FOR CUSTOMERS IN THE UNITED STATES
Uncovered editions are available through all major
wholesalers and bookstores, and are distributed to the
trade by Midpoint Trade Books.
Phone 913 831 2233 for single copy prepaid orders
which can be fulfilled on the spot, or simply for more
information.
Fax 913 362 7401